Routledge Revivals

The Tragedy of Cleopatra Queene of Aegypt by Thomas May

The Tragedy of Cleopatra Queene of Aegypt by Thomas May

Denzell S. Smith

A Critical Edition

First published in 1979 by Garland Publishing, Inc.

This edition first published in 2018 by Routledge
2 Park Square, Milton Park, Abingdon, Oxon, OX14 4RN
and by Routledge
52 Vanderbilt Avenue, New York, NY 10017, USA

Routledge is an imprint of the Taylor & Francis Group, an informa business

© 1979 by Denzell S. Smith

All rights reserved. No part of this book may be reprinted or reproduced or utilised in any form or by any electronic, mechanical, or other means, now known or hereafter invented, including photocopying and recording, or in any information storage or retrieval system, without permission in writing from the publishers.

Publisher's Note
The publisher has gone to great lengths to ensure the quality of this reprint but points out that some imperfections in the original copies may be apparent.

Disclaimer
The publisher has made every effort to trace copyright holders and welcomes correspondence from those they have been unable to contact.

A Library of Congress record exists under ISBN:

ISBN 13: 978-0-367-14888-1 (hbk)
ISBN 13: 978-0-367-14891-1 (pbk)
ISBN 13: 978-0-429-05380-1 (ebk)

A Garland Series

RENAISSANCE DRAMA
A COLLECTION OF CRITICAL EDITIONS

edited by
STEPHEN ORGEL
The Johns Hopkins University

The Tragoedy of Cleopatra Queene of Aegypt
by Thomas May

A Critical Edition

DENZELL S. SMITH

GARLAND PUBLISHING, INC.
NEW YORK & LONDON • 1979

COPYRIGHT © 1979 BY DENZELL S. SMITH

ALL RIGHTS RESERVED

All volumes in this series are printed on
acid-free, 250-year-life paper.

Library of Congress Cataloging in Publication Data
May, Thomas, 1595–1650.
   The tragoedy of Cleopatra, Queene of Aegypt.

   (Renaissance drama)
   Originally presented as the editor's thesis, University
of Minnesota, 1965.
    Bibliography: p.
    Includes index.
    I. Cleopatra, Queen of Egypt, d. 30 B.C.—Drama.
I. Smith, Denzell S. II. Title. III. Series.
PR2709.M3A69   1979   822'.4   78-66784
ISBN 0-8240-9732-7

PRINTED IN THE UNITED STATES OF AMERICA

The Tragedy of Cleopatra Queene of Aegypt.

The Speakers.

Antoniani.	Aegypti.	Caesariani.
Marcus Antonius.	Cleopatra	Caesar Augustus
Marcus Titius.	Eira	Marcus Agrippa
Munatius Plancus.	Charmio	Cornelius Gallus
C. Caninius Crassus.	Achoreus	Pinnarius Scarpus
Caius Sossius.	Euphronius	Proculeius
Titus Domitius.	Seleucus.	Thyrsus
Lucilius.	Glaucus	Epaphroditus
Aristocrates.	Mardio.	

Acted 1626

The Scene Aegypt.

———— quantum impulit Argos
feliciasq; domos facis Spartana nocenti,
Hesperios auxit tantum Cleopatra furores.   Luc

Frontispiece; title page of the manuscript of *Cleopatra*.

THE TRAGŒDY OF CLEOPATRA

QUEENE OF AEGYPT

By

THOMAS MAY

(Written ca. 1626; First Edition 1639)

A CRITICAL EDITION

A THESIS

SUBMITTED TO THE FACULTY OF THE

GRADUATE SCHOOL OF THE

UNIVERSITY OF MINNESOTA

By

Denzell Stewart Smith

IN PARTIAL FULFILLMENT OF THE

REQUIREMENTS FOR THE DEGREE OF

DOCTOR OF PHILOSOPHY

March, 1965

Preface

No earlier edition of this play offers a satisfactory text because an old-spelling critical edition requires a conflation of the author's autograph manuscript and the first printed edition of 1639. Further, this play, while illustrating Caroline skepticism concerning the character of a personage long famous in narrative and dramatic literature as well as in history, departs from the literary tradition of the preceding three centuries. An account of the reasons for its departure invites consideration of its sources, but more important, of the beliefs of the dramatist's contemporaries as shown in both life and literature.

I am grateful to the Librarian of The Huntington Library, San Marino, California, for permission to use a microfilm of the 1639 edition of <u>Cleopatra</u> in preparing the text, and to Professor Huntington Brown for his help in preparing the thesis.

Table of Contents

Preface................................page	iii
Textual Introduction...................	v
Literary Introduction..................	lxxiv
Edited Text............................	1
Appendix 1, Altered Accidentals........	92
Appendix 2, Press Variants.............	95
Appendix 3, Collation of Ms and 1639...	97
Appendix 4, Textual Notes..............	130
Appendix 5, Ms Sentences Ending Within the Line.....	138
Appendix 6, Explanatory Notes..........	148
List of Works Cited....................	174

1. Editions and Scholarship

May's play exists in both manuscript and printed form. The manuscript, British Museum Royal 18 c vii, is briefly described by Warner and Gilson:

> "The Tragoedy of Cleopatra, Queene of Ægypt" [by Thomas May, see Dict. Nat. Biogr.]. The play was acted in 1626, printed in 1639, and again in 1654. With these editions the MS., with a few verbal exceptions, agrees.[1]

Warner and Gilson describe at greater length a fragment of Thomas Ross's continuation of Silius Italicus which appears on the first two leaves of the Cleopatra manuscript in another hand. I have ignored this fragment, although May, like his contemporary Ross, wrote a continuation of a classical peom. May's continuation of Lucan's Pharsalia, which he had translated, gained him considerable contemporary fame.[2] The entire manuscript has 34 folio leaves, measuring 12 1/2 by 7 3/4 inches.[3] The play appeared twice in print in the seventeenth century. The first and only edition published in May's lifetime appeared in 1639, an edition which was reissued with a new title page in 1654, four years after May's death.[4] The title pages of both manuscript and printed edition report that the play was acted in 1626, but the place of performance is not known.[5] The modern edition of the play, a thesis by Sister Mary Ransom Burke done at Fordham in 1943,[6] convincingly presents the evidence for the now nearly century-old assertion first made by the editors of Notes and Queries[7] that 1654 is not a new edition but a re-issue

of 1639 with a new title page. Her collation of five copies of
1639 with two copies of 1654 shows but twenty-four differences
in spelling and no other variants. Most of the spelling differences
are corrections of obvious misspellings in 1639, as, for example,
"friends" for "ftiends." Since 1654 was evidently not revised
by the author and is but a re-issue, it has no substantive authority
and I have not collated it. Sister Mary unfortunately did not
have a copy of the British Museum manuscript for her edition,
probably because it was not available during the second world war.
She did, however, locate copies of the 1639 edition which are
not listed elsewhere. The Union catalogue locates copies at Yale,
the Huntington Library and the Library of Congress;[8] Greg locates
other copies at the British Museum and at the Dyce, Bodleian,
Worcester, Folger, Harvard, and Pforzheimer libraries;[9] the
Short Title Catalogue locates another copy owned by Mr. W. A.
White of New York;[10] and Sister Mary locates copies at the University
of Chicago and the Rosenbach Company of Philadelphia.[11]

Sister Mary's edition of Cleopatra in 1943 presents an
unsatisfactory text. She did not use the British Museum manuscript.
The spelling and punctuation of her text are faithful neither to
the edition of 1639 nor to any one clearly defined set of conventions. She corrects printer's mistakes but does not explain when
or why. She fails to distinguish between a reprint and a critical
edition, and offers no critical or explanatory notes.

Further, in her critical introduction, her tendency to make
ostensibly factual assertions without adequate evidence and later

to reason from such assertions makes for unsound argument, as
where she argues that eighty lines dealing with politics make
the play essentially political in intent.[12] In short, she tries
too hard to prove a thesis.

The only other modern extended study of May's *Cleopatra*,
done by Heinrich Wolfe in 1914, examines the classical sources
of the play, showing May's close adherence to the sources which
the dramatist listed in the margin.[13]

The manuscript of *Cleopatra* was first brought to public
attention by the brief and suggestive survey of seventeenth
century manuscript plays by Bernard Wagner.[14]

Sister M. Simplicia Fitzgibbons's edition of the better of
May's two comedies, *The Old Couple*,[15] offered as a thesis at the
Catholic University in 1943, is no better than Sister Mary's
Cleopatra; indeed it is inferior, because she collated only two
copies of the original edition. However, Sister Simplicia made
a useful contribution by diligently searching out of contemporary
documents explanations of the many allusions and commonplace
beliefs found in the comedy. I should like to have examined a
discussion of May's comedies that was done by Alexander Werner
in 1894, of which I have been unable to locate a copy.[16]

One of May's tragedies, *Julia Agrippina, Empresse of Rome*,
was edited as a thesis in 1914 in an old-spelling reprint,[17] and
Allen Chester's full but sometimes naively expressed biography
of May also was done as a thesis and subsequently published.[18]

May's third tragedy, *The Tragedy of Antigone, the Theban
Princesse* (ca. 1627-1631), has not been edited.

Finally, brief critical notices of May as a dramatist are found in Bentley's *The Jacobean and Caroline Stage*, with a bibliography of May's work,[19] and in Briggs' monograph on the influence of Jonson's tragedy.[20]

2. Editing Principles

From the vantage point of 1964, the modern editions of May's plays which have appeared as doctoral dissertations share the crucial short-coming, because of their early dates, of not using recently developed bibliographical techniques for establishing the text. Their editors offer a text which is nothing more than a diplomatic reprint of the original edition, and only correct minor errors in spelling and punctuation. Schmid's *Agrippina* of 1914 is up-to-date for its time, since he follows the then current practice for old-spelling editions of choosing one copy of one edition for his copy-text and reprinting it with what were then regarded as minor corrections of the accidentals. His edition is a good example of the procedure followed in the series in which it appeared, *Materialien zur Kunde des Älteren Englischen Dramas*, edited by W. Bang. McKerrow's edition of Nashe[21] is a further example of early twentieth-century practice, as is Boas' edition of Kyd.[22] McKerrow's "Note on the Treatment of the Text Adopted in This Edition"[23] precisely describes just what he has done to every detail of the copy he chose as his copy-text. These early twentieth-century editions offered a new critical approach to the problem of reproducing early texts. Their editors chose as the source of

their text an early edition rather than a modern reprint or the last
edition published in the author's lifetime, thereby eliminating the
corruptions that invariably occur in any transmission of a text;
they faithfully reproduced the text in its old-spelling form, thereby
avoiding the knotty problem of partial or complete modernization;
and they laid out for examination the procedures by which they had
arrived at the form of the text. Their practice showed their desire
to present texts in a purer form than had heretofore been done.[24]
These old-spelling texts established a pattern for subsequent serious
editions. McKerrow's practice of choosing the first edition as a
copy-text generally became the rule. The earlier practice had been
to reprint the last edition published in an author's lifetime, since
it supposedly would contain any alterations he might have made.
Montague Summers's edition of the plays of Dryden presents a corrupt
text when, as late as 1933, he followed this principle. Summers's
edition is uncritical because he made no attempt to find out if
alterations were authorial or not, and so avoided the editor's responsibility of determining the authority of his copy-text.[25] As Bowers
says, "The uncritical use of the last edition within an author's lifetime is now, or should be, thoroughly discredited, although it is still
occasionally found."[26] The first edition as copy-text at least avoids
the corruptions that occurred in the author's lifetime, but fails to
include later authorial emendations and offers no means of distinguishing authorial revision from printing house corruption. In the
case of doubtful readings of missing leaves in the copy-text, early

twentieth-century editors collated other copies or later editions
and chose their readings according to the preference of the editor.

Sister Simplicia's edition of May's <u>Old Couple</u> generally
follows the pattern, as does Sister Mary's edition of <u>Cleopatra</u>.
Their editions, however, adopt the further refinement of collating
several copies of one edition in order to locate, if possible,
variants found in one edition. Their collation evidently had
as its aim the discovery of compositors' errors and press-
corrections of these for the purpose of adopting the corrected
reading, although one can only infer their aim since they nowhere
state it. They were, however, on the wrong track in making
their collation since

> the object of the collating of multiple
> copies of a single edition is not to dis-
> cover all known press-corrections in order
> to adopt them. On the contrary, the collation
> should be undertaken in order to discover the
> original readings underneath the usually
> sophisticated press-altered type-setting and
> thus to establish the exact details of the
> original type-setting.[27]

<u>Cleopatra</u> was collated in five copies and <u>The Old Couple</u> in only
two, but partly because of the unrefined state of textual criticism
and partly because of the sparseness of variants in but one
edition, the editors were not able to use the results of their
collation to the greatest advantage. The existence of but one
edition of a play with only a few spelling variants does not
permit the editor to display his bibliographical ingenuity and
provides him with a copy-text which is of necessity authoritative

in both substantive and accidental features. However, in the case
of <u>Cleopatra</u>, compositorial analysis would have established much
about the characteristics of the underlying manuscript. Sister
Mary's edition was a mere reprint of a single authority and not
a critical edition, "which is supposed to present the best detailed
text of an author in a form as close to his intentions as can
be managed."[28] An understanding of the importance of bibliography
for textual criticism was not widespread during the late 1930's
and early 1940's, however, and the editors of May's plays should
not be taken to task for following procedures then current.
Nowadays, however, neither advanced student nor critic ought to
be satisfied with a text that offers anything less than the play
in the form in which the author finally would have presented
it if he had made a fair copy that included all his revisions,
or a text that comes as close as possible to approximating such
a fair copy.[29] Such a text will be an eclectic text.

McKerrow's attempt in 1939 to formulate rules for a critical
edition of Shakespeare displayed the results of his ten years'
experience in trying to edit nine of the plays.[30] His aim was to
reconstruct a text which would resemble an authorial fair copy,[31]
and

> reversing his earlier views, he laid it
> down as his rule ... that, under ordinary
> circumstances, he would select as his copy-
> text the edition closest to the author's
> manuscript and would thereupon incorporate in
> this basic text the substantive alterations
> from any revised edition.[32]

His discussion of the complexities of the problems in editing
Shakespeare unquestionably cleared the way for other textual editors.

In retaining his notion of following one edition as a copy-text,[33] McKerrow encountered difficulties in establishing procedures for choosing the most authoritative reading in the case of alternative readings from different authoritative texts, difficulties which could only be resolved, evidently, by the intuitive sensitivities of the editor.

Greg, in his classic *Editorial Problems in Shakespeare*,[34] insisted on his debt to McKerrow, and did not hesitate to use McKerrow's words while reformulating his rules. Greg bravely advocated an eclectic text[35] which would incorporate in one text the most authoritative readings from different substantive texts. He retained McKerrow's distinction between substantive and derived editions to help establish what reading was authoritative and what was not. A "substantive" edition is one "which cannot have been derived from any other edition now extant" and a "derived" edition is one "derived ... with or without intentional modification, from earlier extant editions. ... It is evident that the 'most authoritative text' of which we are in search must be a 'substantive' one."[36] However, even derived editions can have authority, and an exception to the rule to reprint the copy-text exactly had to be made, Greg felt, "in the event of a later derivative edition being shown to have been corrected or augmented by the author or from some authoritative source."[37] The alternate readings will "have to be treated mainly on their own merits, those only being admitted that can produce satisfactory credentials."[38] Should these corrections be authorial, the editor

> will, while still following the copy-text
> in matters of spelling, punctuation, and the
> like, introduce into it <u>all</u> the alterations of
> the revised edition, other than evident blunders
> and misprints, provided that there is no
> reason to suppose that any of them derive from
> a different and non-authoritative source.[39]

Bowers insists that the chief difference between McKerrow's and Greg's views is in the treatment of the revisions; that the conservative McKerrow would incorporate all substantive alterations from a revised edition while Greg would consider every variant in a revised edition "on its own merits."[40] Greg, he claims, saw "that normal compositor substantive variants could be expected as readily in a revised edition as in a reprint and that these are by no means always so recognizable as are simple misprints or errors."[41] The editor should, therefore, select only the "true revisions." Yet it seems to me that Greg expressly enjoins incorporating into the text all the alterations of a revised edition in the rule quoted above; the difference pointed out by Bowers is an important one, but it must not be conceived to be so by Greg or he would have re-formulated his rule. The difficulty arises over Greg's (and McKerrow's) desire to incorporate all the alternate readings "other than evident blunders and misprints,"[42] and the question to be asked is, "What is an 'evident' blunder?"

Greg's advocacy of an eclectic text was a daring departure because the corrupt texts produced by unprincipled eclecticism (aimed at producing modernized general reading editions) were partly responsible for the new turn-of-the-century critical old-spelling editions. Greg's effort to follow a well-defined principle

in the choice of variants finally hung on a snag. In the case
of variant readings in two substantive editions, Greg faced
a problem that could not be solved by his methods, and he was
forced into saying that

> an editor's choice between alternative readings
> in two substantive editions will ... be determined
> partly by the extrinsic authority of the editions
> and partly by the intrinsic merit of the readings.
> ... His judgement of the readings is, ultimately,
> no doubt, a matter of personal predilection.[43]

Since the aim of twentieth century textual editors has been
to get away from choices involving personal predilection, clearly
an attack had to be made on the problems so carefully pointed
out by Greg. In fact, the attack already had begun in purely
bibliographical studies and in studies of the conditions in the
Elizabethan printing house by such men as Bowers, Hinman, Greg
himself,[44] and the many pioneer studies published during the
century by the Bibliographical Society. The increased attention
paid to textual and bibliographical topics after the second world
war provided information necessary to advances in theory. In
1950, when discussing "The Rationale of Copy-text," Greg re-
affirmed his belief in an eclectic text. He said that McKerrow's
belief that an editor had to make the revised edition the basis
of his reprint was in error, that "this was the old fallacy of
the 'best text,' and may be taken to be now generally rejected."[45]
He rejected the notion because he now clearly saw that an editor
had to distinguish between the substantive matters in a text and
the "accidentals" of spelling, capitalization, and punctuation and
other non-substantive details that provide the "texture" of a text.[46]

His point had been made earlier by McKerrow[47] who did not, however, recognize its importance as Greg himself earlier had not. The distinction is extremely important. For example, it clarifies one of the differences between the editing of classical manuscripts and the editing of early printed dramatic texts, two kinds of editing now recognized as having different procedures[48] but earlier not so recognized, to the confusion of the editors of the dramatic texts. A classical editor concerns himself with the substance of what is said; punctuation, capitalization, and so on are so far removed from the original in the manuscripts he works with that no attempt can be made to recover the practice of the author. In early printed dramatic texts, however, it is sometimes possible to distinguish the author's peculiar orthographical habits beneath the overlay of the compositor, proofreader, and even scribe if there was one. That sixteenth- and seventeenth-century compositors did impose their own characteristics on the accidentals of their copy is as well known as is the author's practice of accepting such changes without complaint.[49] The separation of authorial from compositorial forms is, as Bowers says, "no casual matter,"[50] but the effort does sometimes recover an authentic spelling. For example, the doubtful spelling of Hamlet's "sullied" or "solid" flesh now is correctly established on bibliographical principles as "sullied."[51] Greg's distinction also establishes the "substantive" authority of accidentals, so that we now see that in the case of a play sparsely revised by the author for a second edition the accidentals of the first edition should be preserved and those of the second edition should be ignored, since the compositor of the second edition would impose his characteristic treatment of the accidents on those of the first compositor, thus further departing from the practice of the author.

With Greg's authority and with the advances in bibliographical knowledge, Bowers was in 1958 able to argue powerfully for the separate consideration on bibliographical principles of every variant detail of a text,[52] thereby clarifying Greg's rule that every alteration of a revised edition had to be considered on its own merits but that if the revisions were authorial, then all revisions except obvious errors had to be adopted. Whereas in 1942 Greg fell back on personal predilection in choosing between alternate readings in substantive editions, Bowers in 1958 was able to describe how the authority of several classes of variants in two editions of Dekker's *Honest Whore* could be solved "according to the mechanical evidence of the printing process" so that

> editorial eclecticism in the choice of variants now from one and now from the other edition becomes quite automatic, completely demonstrable, and not subject in the least to differences of critical opinion.[53]

The choice of variants is "automatic" because modern bibliographical techniques enabled Bowers to

> distinguish the use in this second edition of corrected standing type from the first, and of reset type; and then ... to analyze the textual characteristics of the variants in each according to the bibliographical units of the different sheets printed in three different shops.[54]

Old-spelling critical editions are, of course, not the only form in which Elizabethan texts are appearing. The Malone Society, which early formulated "Rules for the Guidance of Editors of the Society's Reprints," recently re-formulated its rules[55] and is still publishing type-facsimile reprints. These reprints serve the good purposes of making accessible otherwise inaccessible texts, of providing an accurate reprint of one copy of the text, and of giving the reader a clear impression of what the original copy looked like. Their disadvantages are in not being useful for bibliographical purposes and in not providing McKerrow's "fair copy." They are reprints of one raw state of the text. A reprint need not be a type-facsimile reprint, of course, as is shown by the recent issue of Sir Thomas Elyot's Of the Knowledge Which Maketh a Wise Man, a page-for-page reprint in modern roman type of the first extant edition.[56] The editor has merely supplied bracketed page numbers, and, for some impression of authenticity, he reproduces display capitals. Modern photographic facsimiles of old texts enable the editor to avoid the problems of reproducing type faces and to avoid the problems of turned letters, obvious errors, and so on, which face every reprint editor; every reader is allowed to be his own textual editor when reading Rich's Farewell to Military Profession in the recent photographic facsimile of the 1581 printed text.[57] The text is not only unsatisfactory on principle, but it is difficult to read because ghost impressions make some pages nearly illegible.

That any reprint of the 1639 edition of May's Cleopatra must be unsatisfactory, whether that reprint be type-facsimile, page-for-page, or photographic, is clear because of the existence of a manuscript (which I shall argue is the author's holograph). I shall try to show that the 1639 edition contains several authorial revisions. Clearly a reprint of the manuscript, while preserving the author's orthographic peculiarities, would not present the revisions he made, and a reprint of 1639, while presenting the revised passages, would not preserve the accidentals of the manuscript. Further, it would in all likelihood contain substantive variants for which the compositor, not the author, would be responsible. The best text for this play is undoubtedly an eclectic text. The matter of old-spelling or a modernized or partially modernized spelling is still hotly argued,[58] but since I have taken as my guiding principle "the restoration of the closest communication between author and reader by removing the barriers of error in the preserved documents,"[59] I have chosen old-spelling. My intention throughout is to present to the reader a text "in which there has been no unnecessary interposition between him and the words of [the] author in their most authoritative form."[60] The "most authoritative form" is meant to include first the words and their arrangement, and second their spelling, punctuation, and capitalization.[61] The rationale of such an old-spelling critical edition has been ably made by the theoretical discussions of McKerrow, Greg, and Bowers, and by the practice of textual critics and editors like

Hinman, Philips, and, of course, Greg and Bowers.

3. The Choice of the Copy-Text

The argument for the validity of the manuscript as the copy-text, while somewhat involved and detailed, has as its main points, first, that the manuscript represents a fair copy of the play with minor authorial revisions; second, that the manuscript precedes the printed play in date; third, that the printed play has as its source a manuscript similar to mine but revised for the printer; fourth, that the substantive changes in the printed play are generally authorial; and fifth, that the manuscript has been subjected to house- or compositorial styling of accidentals. It follows that the text must be established by a conflation of the manuscript and the printed play.

The Manuscript a True Copy

If the minor revisions made within the manuscript can be shown to be authorial, then the manuscript must have been carefully read by the author and so can be said to be a true copy of the play in the form the author then intended to present it. The non-substantive revisions show a careful attention to details; substantive revisions show a careful attention to phrasing; and, in my opinion, the handwriting of the play and the handwriting of the revisions is the same, although on the latter point expert opinion is not as complete as it might be.

The non-substantive revisions are of three kinds, corrections of smeared ink, corrections of spelling, and corrections of false starts. The non-substantive revisions are chiefly useful in my argument to show that someone paid careful attention to the details of the text.

Five corrections of smears occur, and in each case the correction is written just above the smeared place. For example, at III iii 45 "men" is blurred and the word written again above it; at II iii 2 the third "c" in "circumstances" is smeared and written above; and at I i 132 the "r" in "Masters" is smeared and written above. Such details only show that care was taken that the copy be legible; and since all five corrections are made above blurred but still legible letters, the copyist was clearly at pains to be careful.

Non-substantive spelling corrections also show careful attention to detail. Four of them are corrections of obvious errors: "enterpose" for "entepose" at II iii 23; "fooles" for "foles" at III iii 12 (the word occurs twice in the manuscript line, spelled "fooles" the first time); "good" for the first written "god" at III iii 106 (in the address "Doo good my Lord"); and "what" for "hat" at IV ii 24. Two attempts to correct spelling remain blurred. In the command "<u>Thyreus</u> come hither" at III ii 80, the word "hither" evidently is intended to replace the first written "higher," since the bold scrambled pen strokes of the written in "t" cover the finer lines of the "g." The word "frendshipp" at V ii 57 has the "f" and "r" written over with successive strokes and the "e" is written above what might be an "a." All three letters are somewhat blurred.

The third class of non-substantive revisions is the corrections of false starts. Five revisions correct ordinary scribal errors. The copyist first wrote and scratched out "wi" at the beginning of the sentence "My wishes are effected" (II iii 105), thereby correcting a transposition; he wrote "when" at the end of a line rather than properly as the first word of the next line (II iv 54), another transposition; he first wrote a long "s" rather than the "T" which he scratched over it in the word "Tall" in the line "Were Tall, and slowly did like castles moove" (III i 56), a shifting of letter corrected; after writing "to give" he next correctly wrote "to" but then a "g" as the first letter of the next word rather than the correct "C" of "Cæsar's" (V iii 97), correcting a repetition; and, after writing the stage direction "Exit Proculeius" at III ii 20-21, he first wrote the stage direction two lines later as "Enter Procul," but cancelled "Procul" to correctly write "Euphronius" on the same line, again correcting a repetition. Three corrections are considerably more interesting because they could count as evidence for the copyist being the author. The word "And" is cancelled as the first word in the line "What ruine lesse then Chaos shall involve" (II iv 6). "And" does not occur as a word in any position in a nearby line; the copyist merely might have erred, or he might have intended to write something else. The end parenthesis was first written and then scratched out after the word "else" in the lines "(fearing it

seemes to bee excluded else / From her owne kingdome)" (III ii 4-5).
This might be a case of eyeskip, but it also might show the
author first intending to end the parenthesis after "else,"
a perfectly logical place in the context to end it, but then
deciding to be more specific and tell what the Queen feared to
be excluded from. Third, a long "s" was first written and then
the upper case "M" of "Master" written over it in the lines

> hee oft would say
> Hee ow'd a better beeing to his Master
> Then to his father; one meere naturall
> The other mentall, and diviner farre.
>   IV ii 14-17

Cæsar is describing how Julius Cæsar honored his teacher.
Could the word "servant" have been planned and cancelled?
Finally, twenty-one minor mistakes and pen slips are corrected.
For example, the "ru" of "distrust" is written over a heavily
cancelled spot which might be an "a" (IV i 77); two letters
are heavily scratched over between the words "and" and "state"
in the line "Great <u>Julius</u> noble acts in warre and state" (I
i 43); a letter is heavily scratched out between the words "Empire,
craves" (V v 90); and a letter is heavily scratched out preceding
the first word in the part-line "'Twas the Aspe." (V v 79).

While the evidence of the non-substantive manuscript
revisions only peripherally supports the validity of the manuscript as the copy-text, the details do show that the copyist
quite carefully corrected his work, an assertion which is also
supported by the generally homogenous texture of the accidentals
in the manuscript and the careful pointing of the manuscript.

Only rarely does the pointing of the manuscript need emendation, and, in comparison to the pointing of the 1639 edition, it is admirably consistent and logical. While discussing the possible validity of a revised reprint as the copy-text, Greg asserts that

> It is ... rather such detailed supervision [as that of Ben Jonson to his revised folio of 1616] than the introduction of textual alterations that justifies our ranking a revised reprint as a substantive edition.[62]

Now while the manuscript of *Cleopatra* is not a "revised reprint," nor a print of any kind, Greg's comment is useful in that it shows the importance he attaches to "detailed supervision" in deciding on whether a text has substantive authority or not. My contention is that the close attention to detail shown by the reviser of the manuscript helps show first, that the manuscript is the proper text to choose for a copy-text, and second, that only the author would so carefully pay attention to detail. However, the substantive and semi-substantive revisions of the manuscript more directly support the first assertion of my argument, that the manuscript represents a fair copy of the play with minor authorial revisions. This class of revisions will be divided into two parts, those revisions made because of meter, and those made because of the sense.

The blank verse of May's play is regular throughout, except for three uses of three stressed lines (at I ii 151, III i 19, and III i 32-34). An author who desired regularity would, when making minor revisions, straighten out any lapses that

he noticed. Four revisions regularize the meter. The copyist
first wrote "They still remain'd encampd, and though oft" (III i 83),
but then placed an inferior caret between the "p" and "d" of
"encampd" to show the superior addition of an "e", thus making
the line regular: "They still remain'd encamped, and though
oft." Conversely, elision in "rained" guaranteed the regularity
of the line first written as "It rained whole showers of
blood, whose colour sett." The "e" of "rained" was replaced
by an apostrophe (II iv 86). A midline lapse was regularized
when the line "Her spatious kingdome, and neighbour-Princes" was
revised to "Her spatious kingdome, and all neighbour-Princes"
(I i 71). Fourth, the line "No, no Girles, I will bee still
myself" is regularized to "No, no my Girles, I will bee still
myselfe" (V v 38). The unstressed syllable missing early in
the unrevised line is supplied in the revision. The remaining
revision in this class was also probably made to straighten
out the meter, but it is not as successful in doing so as the
preceding examples. The copyist first wrote "No other sect
but thine; I am a Timonist" (III iii 14). The last two syllables
of "Timonist" must be slurred together to make a regular
weak ending. But the copyist struck out the word "other,"
thereby enforcing regularity by allowing only ten syllables,
but placing a heavy stress on the ordinarily weakly stressed
last syllable of "Timonist." Since the reviser succeeded quite
well in regularizing four of the five lines, and since the blank
verse elsewhere tends to a metronone-like regularity (except
for the three passages irregular in length but regular in

meter noted above, barring III i 33 which begins with a trochee), the revisions of meter show that the reviser attempted to bring the irregular lines into conformity with the rest of the play. Except for the possibility that the irregularities of meter were intended to serve a poetic purpose (which patently they were not), the odds are that only the author himself would be concerned enough about a handful of irregular lines in a full length play to revise them. If we were to grant that the revisions of meter are authorial, a number of inferences can be made about the dramatist, none of them very flattering: for example, his insistence on observing the beat shows that he values regularity for its own sake, and that regularity might be valued over apt expression; his lack of variety in meter shows an inability to achieve freedom of expression in an established form and a temperament hidebound by technique. In short, he must be somewhat dull and unimaginative, a poet on the lowest slopes of Parnassus. He sounds suspiciously like the author of the unrevised lines of the play.

The revisions of lines for the sense is perhaps the most important sub-class of revisions to support the assertion that the manuscript can be regarded as a revised, true copy. The revisions of sense are of two kinds, those which clearly change the meaning, and those which add words obviously omitted by the copyist.

Eight of the revisions of the meaning could have been made either while the author was making a true copy of the play

or while he proofread a true copy. They all change but one word.
In the lines listed below, the word in brackets is the cancelled
but still legible word:

1. To have [take] his share, and, as hee did in
   in power, I i 57

2. Ambition would [will] are long find out a cause
   I i 121

3. It moov'd [flew] directly upwards, II iv 20

4. Nor willingly lett Cleopatra dy [goe] III ii 63

5. No spite [storme] of fortune that shee has
   endur'd, III iii 132

6. That kill with speede [ease] . No easy way to
   death   IV i 2

7. (Whilest thou preferring forreine love [warre]
   before V ii 55

8. I then [still] with best persuasions strove to
   winne her, V ii 82

A purpose for most of the revisions can be discerned. In the
first line, Canidius is describing how Julius Caesar came to his
power; "have" is more flattering to Caesar's greatness (fixed
to him by the epithet "great" in I i 56) than is "take." In
the second line, the indicative mode of "will" too knowingly
suggests as existing fact what only might happen in the future,
a condition better stated by the subjunctive mode. Further, the
change makes the verb agree in mode with the verb of the preceding
line. In the third line "moov'd" more accurately describes what
a comet, the antecedent of "it," does than "flew." In the fourth
line, the reviser again makes the line more precise since Caesar
is describing what he wants to do with Cleopatra:

> I would not loose this gold;
> Nor willingly lett Cleopatra dy
> Before her person have adorn'd my triumph.
> III ii 62-64

To merely let her "goe" is too indefinite an end; to prolong her end for vanity's sake while knowing full well what that end will be does much to characterize the young Cæsar. In the fifth line, presumably "storme" was changed to avoid what must have been a cliché. In the sixth line "case" more than likely was cancelled to avoid repetition. In the seventh line, the antecedent of "thou" is Antony, and Cæsar more correctly describes Antony's activities just before their battles with the word "love" than he did with the word "warre." In the eighth line, a subordinate describes to Cæsar how he tried to persuade Cleopatra to surrender. He begins:

> Wee came and call'd at <u>Cleopatraes</u> tombe.
> Whoo from above made answere, and deny'd
> To yeild herselfe but upon <u>Cæsar's</u> word.
> I then [still] with best persuasions
> strove to winne her...   V ii 79-82

Since he has not described his persuasions at length in the lines preceding the revised line, he is not justified in using "still" and the revision is sensible.

The word "sensible" can indeed be applied to most of these eight revisions. Once again the revisions show a careful but unimaginative workman ironing out minor difficulties. More interesting from the point of view of an editor are four substantive revisions that perhaps show the author as copyist. The revision of IV ii 31-32 is made in this fashion in the manuscript:

> Antonius is strong,—a̶n̶d̶ in well provided
> And skillful horsemen, and despaire of favour....

The change is a correction of a false start of what appears to be the first intended reading

> Antonius is strong, and well provided
> In skillful horsemen, and despaire of favour....

Surely the explanation is that we have here the author himself writing "Antonius is strong, and well provided," but then immediately the writer seeing that this would be virtually saying the same thing twice, puts "in" in place of "and" and at once goes on to make "well provided" modify "horsemen," where it expresses a particular and interesting idea (well accoutred cavalry), and not a mere tautology. Further evidence for the author composing is found in the following revision.

>   kinde of
> What˄mischeife is it G̶o̶d̶d̶e̶s̶? oh yes Godds
>   II iv 8

Two reasons for the change can be found. First, it makes the meter regular, avoiding the irregularity of either a six-foot line missing one unstressed syllable; or, if "oh" be read as metrically unstressed, the slight irregularity is that of an extra unstressed syllable in an otherwise regular five foot line. More likely, however, is his noticing that the repetition of the word "Godds" was undesirable, chiefly because its use in the question detracts from its force in the exclamation. Such a detail would be noticed by a person making a fair copy after the line was written, and the revision would be made by inserting and cancelling. Stronger evidence for the author composing is found in the revision of III ii 7:

> Her s̶e̶l̶f̶e̶ shipps all crown'd with laurell,
>   to deceive

A copyist might, without looking carefully enough at his copy, write "selfe" after the word "her," because in this case the word "selfe" makes sense if read in the line instead of "shippe":

> Her selfe all crown'd with laurell, to
>   deceive...

It is perfectly in character for Cleopatra to deceitfully adorn her self. The word "shippe" is, however, more suitable, since the populace of Alexandria would more quickly get the false news if the ships entered the harbor so draped, decoration on such a scale might effectively convey a strong impression of a great victory, and finally, if the ships so draped followed Cleopatra's into the harbor, the true news would not be known until she was safely ashore. That the revision is not superposed but is made on the same line shows that the copyist crossed out "selfe" and inserted "shipps." Surely the arguments favor the author making such a change. The final revision of the sense occurs when Cleopatra frees a prisoner from the death penalty:

>   oure
> Doom'd by the law ~~of~~ royall pardon frees thee.
>   IV i 56

Once again, a copyist might naturally write the word "of" after "law" because the sequence of words is common. But even more likely is the possibility that this conventional and mediocre author, while making a fair copy, was about to write the expected sequence "law of Egypt," "law of royall Egypt," or "law of royall Cleopatra," and while writing the line saw how he could more economically say what he meant. All he really need say is "the law;" since the scene is Cleopatra's court, and she has summoned two prisoners awaiting the death penalty to try out her poisons, obviously the law is

Egypt's or hers.

    The last class of substantive revisions are those which add to the line omitted or overlooked words necessary to the sense. Four examples occur, and in each case the place where the addition is to be made is shown by an inferior caret and the word is written in a superscript position.

1. When wee have _^ the substance, is best kept
   (lost)
                                          I i 114

2. His rough and cruell _^ and made him learne
   (soule)
                                         I ii 73

3. May call thee mistress of _^ subject world.
   (the)
                                      II iii 34

4. That love is true that's shew'd _^ misery.
   (in)
                                        V iii 94

Such revisions could have been made by a copyist looking over his line just after he wrote, but the first example might easily have been missed since the line makes grammatical sense (though involving metrical irregularity) but not a sense that is consistent with the thought of either speaker. The insertions could also have been made by the copyist while writing the line, when he would realize that he had forgotten a word. This class of substantive revisions again shows the attention to detail of the copyist, since nowhere in the manuscript are there gross lapses in the sense, and even these few errors have been corrected.

    While only one revised line counts heavily as evidence for the author as the copyist (the substitution of "shipps" for "selfe"), a fair amount of evidence reasonably suggests that the revisions might be authorial, and no contrary evidence whatsoever is to be found

What woman Antony enioyes? haue wee
Time to dispute his matrimoniall faults
That haue already giuen the breach of all
Romes sacred lawes, by which the world was bound?
Haue wee endur'd ours Consuls state and power
To see subiected by the lawlesse armies
Of priuate men, oure Senatours proscrib'd?
And can wee now consider whither they
That did all this, may keepe a wrench or no?
It was the crime of vs and fate it selfe
That Antony and Cæsar could vsurpe
A power so great, beyond which wee can suffer
No more worth thinking of, nor nere't to vs
Any great fortune if Antonius
Were honest of his body? Ple: haue wee then,
Whoe haue beene greatest Magistrates, quite lost
All shew of libirty, and now not dare
To counsell him?
Ca: a show of libirty
When wee haue lost the substance, is oist kept
By seeming not to vnderstand those faults
Which wee want power to mend. for mine owne part
I loue the person of Antonius,
And through his greatest loosenesse can discerne
A nature freer, honester then Cæsar's.
And if a warr should grow twixt them (as surely
Ambition will ere long find out a cause
Although Octauia had not beene neglected)
Rather then Rome should serue since two Lords
Could wish that all were Antony's alone.
Whoe would, I thinke, bee brought more easily
Then Cæsar, to resigne the gouernment.
Ple: would I could thinke that either would doo so.
Enter Marcio.

Figure 1. Manuscript page 5v, showing two revisions.

The Tragedie

Her spacious Kingdomes, and all neighbour Princes
Admire her parts. How many languages
Speaks she with elegancest Embassadors
From th' Æthiopians, Arabs, Troglodites,   *Plut.*
From th' Hebrews, Syrians, Medes, and Parthians
Have in amazement heard this learned Queen
Without the aid of an interpreter
In all their severall tongues returne their answers;
When most of her dull predecessor Kings
Since *Ptolomæus Philadelphus* time
Scarce understood th' Ægyptian tongue, and some
Had quite forgot the Macedonian.
          TI.
How well *Canidius* descants on this theame!
          PLA.
I'll lay my life it pleases him; the man
Is deep in love, and pity tis he has
So great a rivall as *Antonius*.
          CA.
Well use your wit upon me, but I doubt
If any man could search your secret thoughts,
'Tis envy, not morality that makes
You taxe his love, how gravely ere you talke.
          TI.
But can *Canidius* think it should be just
In our *Antonius* to forsake for her
His lawfull wife the good *Octavia*?
          CA.
Then like a Roman let me answer, *Martius*.
Is it become a care worthy of us
What woman *Antony* enjoy'd, have we
Time to discusse his matrimoniall faults,
That have already seen the breach of all
Romes sacred laws, by which the world was bound?
Have we endur'd our Consuls state and power
To be trampled by the lawlesse arms

of CLEOPATRA.

Of private men, or Senators proscrib'd,
And can we now consider whether they
That did all this, may keep a wench or no?
It was the crime of us, and Fate it self
That *Antony* and *Cæsar* could usurpe
A power so great; beyond which we can suffer
No more worth thinking of. Nor were't to us
Any great fortune if *Antonius*
Were honest of his body.
          PLA.
Have we then,
Who have been greatest Magistrates, quite lost
All shew of liberty, and now not dare
To counsell him?
          CA.
A shew of liberty
When we have lost the substance, is best kept
By seeming not to understand those faults
Which we want power to mend. For mine own part
I love the person of *Antonius*,
And through his greatest loosenesse can discern
A nature here, honester then *Cæsars*.
And if a warre do grow twixt them (as surely
Ambition would ere long finde out a cause
Although *Octavia* had not been neglected)
Rather then Rome should still obey two Lords,
Could wish that all were *Anthony's* alone.
Who would, I think, be brought more easily
Then *Cæsar*, to resigne the government.
          TI.
Would I could think that either would do so.
Here comes her servant *Mardio*.   *Enter* Mardio.
          MAR.
Noble Lords,
The Queen by mee entreats your company
At supper with the Lord *Antonius*.

Figure 2.   Sig. B3, 1639 edition, showing manuscript
revisions included in the printed text.
(Reproduced by permission of The Huntington
Library, San Marino, California).

in the particulars so far examined. The evidence reasonably well supports the assertions that the reviser of the manuscript paid close attention to the important details of making smeared places quite clear, of correcting obvious misspelling, and of adding omitted words necessary to the sense. He also concerned himself with verse technique by generally successfully revising irregular lines. Finally his brief substantive revisions, while not brilliant, generally improve the line and the reason for the revision is clear. All substantive revisions of the manuscript appear in the 1639 edition (compare figure one to figure two), except where the whole passage is revised for 1639. Were these revisions not the author's, it is doubtful if they would have found their way into the printer's copy which must have been scrutinized and approved by the author.

Not only do these assertions support the view that the manuscript is a revised fair copy, but they help show that the reviser was the copyist. But what of the handwriting? In my opinion, the hand in which the revisions are made is the same hand found in the rest of the manuscript, a hand for the most part Italian but retaining certain characteristics of the secretary hand. The general appearance of the revisions resembles that of the rest of the text, and when the letters and combinations of letters of the revised words are carefully compared to similar letters and combinations elsewhere in the text, they appear to be identical (see figures one and three). Evidently no specimen of May's handwriting has been reproduced.[63] In their description of the manuscript

> nor, oh no, my Lord, shee loues you as her life.
> No spite of fortune that shee has endur'd,
> Or can hereafter feare, greiues her so much
> As doese your absence and strange melancholy.
> Ari: well Ma[r]io thou art fitter for this place.
> Ca: my Lord Antonius. An: ha! more men upon us!
> Ca: J come to bring thee heauy newes, Antonius.
> The forces all, which thou didd'st leaue incamp'd
> At Actium horse and foot are gone to Cæsar.
> And all th' auxiliary kings. no strength
> At all is left thee, but what heere thou hast
> At Alexandria. An: ha! La: this sinkes into him.
> Ca: it makes a deepe impression in his passion
> Ari: and may perchance expell his other fit.
> Ant: all you here yett! then J haue freinds / he
> But tell mee can you bee so mercifull
> As to forgiue that most inhumane fitt
> J haue euer in! oh J am all in clusters.
> Ca: my Lord take better comfort. Ant. dearest freind
> J will nere profess against any fortune now.
> come, let's together to the court, and there   Plutarch.
> Drowne sad'nesse in rich cuppes of Meroe wine,
> And laugh at Fortunes malice; for your sight
> More cheeres my spirits then her frownes can dull them.   exeunt.

Actus Quartus.

Cleopatra, Glaucus.

> Gl: Madam, all druggs with paine and torment kill,
> That kill with speede. no easy way to death

Figure 3. Manuscript page 21r, showing two revisions.

copy of May's poem The Reigne of King Henry the second, written in
seven bookes, Warner and Gilson say that "the hand of the corrector
of a few words ... seems to be that of the corrector of the same
author's 'Cleopatra'."[64] I sent to the British Museum for photostats of revised leaves of the Reigne of King Henry, hoping either
that the revisions would be extensive enough to make a close
comparison possible, or to prove the hand of the copyist of King
Henry the same hand as that of the copyist of the unrevised
portions of Cleopatra. The photostats were disappointing on both
counts. The revisions in King Henry are very infrequent one word
insertions, and the three leaves I ordered show but one inserted
word per leaf (see figures four and five). More disappointing was
the professional-appearing hand in which the text of   Henry
appears. The copyist approximates a printed title page, duplicates
italic type, and writes a clear hand much like printed letters
on ruled paper. In two ways, however, Warner and Gilson's statement
supports my assertion that May was probably the copyist of Cleopatra.
First, their expert opinion is that the hands of the correctors seem
to be the same, and if the same, the odds are that only the author
would so carefully revise both manuscripts. Second, the manuscript
of King Henry provided no contrary evidence. In the absence of
such evidence, who else could be responsible? However, Warner and
Gilson's statement is in one way confusing. They clearly say that the
corrector's hands appear to be the same. They do not say that the
corrector's hand of King Henry is the same hand that wrote the
text of Cleopatra, nor do they say that the corrector of Cleopatra
also wrote the entire manuscript. Their description of the manu-

Booke 1

Of Englands King, such moderation hee
Had shew'd, so rul'd his power with equity,
Seeking no lawlesse and vniust encrease,
That Europe then possest a happy peace.
This peace when fierce Enyo had beheld,
And saw all seedes of warre and faction queld,
Shee sigh'd and wept, for nought could pleasing bee
To that dire mayde but warres calamity;
Nought but dissention did to her seeme good,
No sights but feilds and rivers stain'd with blood
Were her delightsome prospects: into aire
Shee mounts, and fill'd with fury and despaire
Shakes as shee flyes, her now-extinguish'd brand,
Which giues no blaze at all, then taking stand
About the shore of fruitfull Normandy
Vpon a lofty cliffe veiwes from on high
Great Henry's large dominions, that extend
From Scotland Northward to the Southerne end
Of wealthy France, which those high mountaines bound
Nam'd from Pyrenes death, ore all that ground
Shee sees, and gnashes for disdaine to see,
No streaming Ensignes, no hostility.
The murdrous swords to sythes were turn'd agayne,
And cheerefull plowmen till the fertile plaine,
The heardsmen heare theire bullocks gently Lough,
And theire owne feilds the fearelesse shepheards know

Figure 4.   Manuscript p. 10, *King Henry*, showing one revision.

Booke 2.

Of royalty, the power and Regall sway
Nothing (alas) this coronation day
Has brought thee to, but to a nearer sight
Of what thou hast not, nor is yett thy right.
Thy stirring minde meetes torture with a throne,
But Fantalized in dominion.
The cause, alas, of woes that must ensue,
And thy great father too too soone shall rue.

    That dayes solemnity in truest state
The court of England strove to celebrate,
And with such great magnificence, as might
The Maiesty of that high presence fitt:
Where all at once three Kings, two Queenes were mett,
Besydes so many high-borne Princes, great
In fame and wealth, the feasting boords were fill'd
With what this Iland or rich France could yeild.
Such cates as those, with which old Poets fain'd
In Thessaly the Gods were entertain'd
At siluer-footed Thetis bridall feast,
Where Ioue himselfe vouchsaf'd to bee a guest.
Where aged Chiron waited at the bord,
And brought what aire, earth, waters could afford.
When all rich Tempe, and the adioyning seas
Were search'd, besides what then the Naiades,
What young Palæmon, Glaucus, and the greene
Sea-nymphs had brought to grace theire beauteous Queene.

                                                The

Figure 5. Manuscript page 28, <u>King Henry</u>, showing one revision.

script of Cleopatra[65] disappointingly makes no mention of the similarity or dissimilarity between the hand of the copyist and that of the reviser. But once again there is no contrary evidence. Probability suggests that May made the surviving manuscript of his own play.

The Manuscript Precedes the Printed Play in Date

In order for the manuscript to be regarded as the copy-text, it must be shown by internal evidence to be earlier in date than the 1639 edition since no external evidence of its date exists. Were external evidence to show the manuscript of a later date, its authority would be doubtful and the problems that would then arise would be baffling. However, the manuscript cannot be regarded as later.

Sister Mary convincingly shows that the so-called 1654 edition of May's Cleopatra is not a new edition at all, but a reissue of the 1639 sheets with a new title page.[66] Her findings lend support to the earlier date of the manuscript because few men would willingly transcribe an already printed, not sold out, unknown play by a writer not well known as a dramatist, and also because no writer would have a manuscript copy made of an inferior version of his play, even though, as Greg asserts, carefully written manuscripts were more valued than printed copies in the Elizabethan age.[67]

Though by and large inferior to the manuscript, the 1639 edition contains several passages of improved clarity or adequacy of expression and translation. A few typical examples of each kind of improvement will exemplify the statement. An improvement is made in the last line of this speech:

> For should <u>Octavia</u> enterpose herself
> In this great warre (as once before shee did)
> And make them frends, that end to mee were fatall.

when the last line is expanded in 1639 to two lines:

> And make her brother, and her husband friends
> Wher's <u>Cleopatra</u> then? But here he comes.
>   II iii 25-26

The pronoun "them" in the manuscript reading "and make them frends" is intended to refer to Antony and Cæsar, but the manuscript sentence is constructed so that the pronoun can also refer to a reunion of the estranged Octavia and Antony. The 1639 reading corrects this difficulty as well as provides an entrance cue. A second improvement of expression is found in the revision of IV i 145-146. The manuscript lines claim that Cæsar

> Besides that greatnesse which the world adores
> Brings such a freshnesse both of youth and beauty...

but 1639 says that Cæsar

> Besides that power and greatnesse, which the
>   world
> Both knows and fears, brings such a youth and
>   beauty ....

The 1639 reading seems to me superior since the world seldom "adores" "greatnesse," and since all of manuscript line 146 describes the comparatively inconsequential matter of Cæsar's age and appearance while 1639 puts proper attention on Cæsar's stature. Several of the revisions try to make entrances and exits smoother. For example, I ii opens with servants preparing a feast for Antony and Cleopatra. The manuscript abruptly breaks off their small talk by the sudden announcement "but hearke they come," (I ii 13) followed by the stage direction "A flourish" and the entrance of the revellers. The revision makes the entrance smoother by rounding off their preparations:

>   But art thou sure
>   That all things here are well?
>   Ch.   As exquisite
>   As the Queen's wish would have it. Hark
>   they come.   I ii 13-15

Finally, the departure of Thyreus at IV i 171-172 is made less abrupt in the revision. The manuscript has

>   Thy.   I will be ready to attend youre highnesse.
>   Exit Thyreus.

The 1639 edition, however, expands the passage to:

>   Thy.   I will attend your highnesse.
>   Cle.   Till anone
>   Farewell, good Thyreus: but be neer about us.
>   Exit Thyreus.

Generally speaking, however, most of the revisions do not make startling improvements of the text. But a handful of revisions are for more than one line, and no major overhaul of whole speeches or passages is made. Most of the revisions are minor changes of a word or two, showing minor improvement. Such an attempt at general minor improvement is probably the work of an author satisfied with his work but giving it a final careful going-over before delivering the copy to the printer.

The 1639 Edition Set Up From a Manuscript Similar to the Copy-Text

That the printed play depended for its source on a manuscript similar to that used as my copy-text can be seen in the handling of accidentals of sentences ending within the line within a speech in the 1639 edition. Changes of address occurring within a line do not provide evidence for this argument. The differences in these accidentals in the manuscript and in the 1639 edition show that the printer's copy was nearly identical in pointing and capitalization to the copy-text manuscript, and further, the compositor's misreading of the passage at III ii 50-53 corroborates the evidence of the mid-line punctuation.

The details of the differences in accidentals of sentences ending within the line have been recorded in Appendix 5. When the manuscript and 1639 agreed, no entry was made. In 48 lines, the accidentals of punctuation and capitalization were treated in identical ways. In 185 lines, differences in pointing and capitalization exist. At two places where an upper case letter is normal, the copyist habitually used a lower case letter. First, except for proper nouns, the first letter of the first word following a speech prefix was written in lower case by the copyist. The copyist placed speech-prefixes at the left margin and followed the prefix by a colon. The compositor regularly raised the lower case letter following a speech prefix to upper case, because he centered the speech prefixes above the line, and so conventionally began every line with a capital letter. Second, when a sentence ends within the line, and is followed by another sentence within an address, the copyist wrote a lower case letter as the first letter of the first word of a new address, except when that word was a proper noun, when he conventionally used an upper case letter. His practice in this matter is consistent throughout the manuscript, and his practice caused considerable difficulty in the printing house. Clearly no proofreader sat down with the manuscript and methodically corrected the capitalization of these sentences because the printed copy shows no particular consistency in its handling of these accidentals. From first to last, variety exists, but the most common way of solving the problem is to change the end punctuation of the sentence from the clearly written full stop of the manuscript to a comma, semi-colon, or colon, effecting a comma splice or other artificial joining of clauses, thus confusing the syntax in an effort to cope with the orthography of the copyist. In other cases, the full stop is retained but the first letter of the next word raised to upper case, the punctuation is ignored, or the practice of the copyist is followed.

The following table describes the compositor's practice act by act. Not reported by the table are two instances of possible turned letters or broken type: at III iii 105 and V ii 68 the collation is "perpetuity. but] perpetuity·but"; "it. well] it· well." Either 1639 has in each case a turned letter, or a colon has the bottom part broken off and was used twice. I did not count these examples in my tabulations.

Two matters are not described by the table. First, it appears that either the compositor or proofreader began working on the play with the intention of normalizing the mid-line punctuation to printing house standards. In I i, six out of seven lower case letters beginning sentences are raised to upper case and the final punctuation retained; in I ii six out of fifteen are raised and retained, and in II i only two out of ten are raised and retained. Thereafter this kind of

The 1639 Edition's Treatment of the Manuscript's Final Punctuation
and Capitalization of Sentences Ending Within the Line Followed
by a New Sentence but no Change of Address

Act	MS and 1639 identical	Change end punct. to comma	Change end punct. to semi-colon	Change end punct. to colon	Retain MS final punct. & raise next letter to u.c.	Use no punct. & retain l.c.	Totals by act
I	8	4	3	2	12	1	22
II	10	8	7	6	5	0	26
III	15	7	17	13	7	0	44
IV	10	9	8	20	8	0	43
V	5	12	10	20	7	1	49
Totals by kind	48	40	43	61	39	2	184

revision is intermittent. The second matter not described by
the table is the curious practice of normalizing the first few
instances in each act except Act II. In Act I, the first three
instances are raised and retained, in Act II the compositor
changes punctuation, in Act III the first instance is raised
and retained, in Act IV the first two instances are raised and
retained, and in Act V the first three instances are raised and
retained. This pattern might be due to chance, but more than
likely a half-hearted attempt was made to normalize and was
then dropped.

The evidence of Appendix 5 organized in the table also
shows an effort on the part of proofreader or compositor to
normalize the mid-line lower case letter beginning a sentence.
Notice that in Act I, while but 22 instances of change occur,
12 of them raise the first letter to upper case. In Act II,
commas, semi-colons and colons are used about equally to join
clauses in 21 of the 26 changes. In Act III more semi-colons
and colons are used than before, as the number of changes increases
to 44. Acts IV and V show an increased use of colons over other
methods of solving the problem. The scant use of the device
of simply using no punctuation at all where the manuscript has
a full stop appears only twice in the play, and probably is not
a device but an omission. While only two instances occur, this
evidence strongly suggests that the compositor's copy resembled
the manuscript because by failing to notice the full stop in
his copy he would continue to set the line as it appears in the

manuscript, with no upper case letter at the beginning of a
sentence in mid-line. That neither compositor nor proofreader
noticed the omission is shown by the distortion of sense caused
by the omission of final punctuation in the lines in 1639:

> <u>Munatius Plancus</u> in this whole discourse
> Thou speak'st my very thoughts no more,
> here comes
> Lucilius, whither so fast?   I ii 228-230

The manuscript has a full stop after "thoughts." An edition that
has in it 40 comma splices, 43 independent clauses joined by
semi-colons, 61 independent clauses joined by colons, and 2 lines
which omit mid-line punctuation and capitalization, with each of
these splices, joinings, or omissions corresponding to an
unconventional spelling practice in my copy-text, must have been
set from a manuscript copy of the play nearly identical in
appearance to my manuscript.

However, two passages present disparate evidence. In
these passages, my manuscript joins clauses by semi-colons,
but 1639 makes separate sentences (of; nor] of. Nor   I i 108;
returne; until] return. Untill   III i 86). Either the semi-
colons were revised to full stops in the printer's copy and he
raised the following lower case letter, or paradoxically, the
compositor reversed his usual procedure. The first explanation
is more likely, and the further possibilities exist that the copyist erred and transcribed a period for a semi-colon, or the
compositor misread a semi-colon for a full stop. Since explanations can be found for the existence of but two disparate
instances, they do not, I think, detract from the validity of my

hypothesis about the printer's copy closely resembling my manuscript.

One question remains. Why did the compositor choose to revise in different ways the regular practice of the copyist? Why not follow the practice of normalizing suggested by his consistency in I i, or follow the practice of the copy-text as he did 48 times? First, I think that his intention was to normalize in the way suggested by his practice in I i, but the intention was not carried out. Since the learned authorities suggest that a compositor had considerable freedom in spelling and punctuation, perhaps he was left to solve the problems as he saw fit, or, if a proofreader was responsible for the changes, he made revisions as he saw fit. As Bowers says,

> we no longer believe in such hypotheses as that a distinctive house-style was imposed upon a manuscript as a matter of policy by an Elizabethan printer; but we do know that a compositor was sure to overlay some of his own personal characteristics upon a text, and the proofreader some of his own too.[68]

In my opinion the great number of changes in midline punctuation are compositorial, and the occasional efforts to normalize the chaos caused by the changes are due to the proofreader. But because "it is clear that the usual Elizabethan proofreader did not consult copy regularly, if at all,"[69] he soon abandoned the effort because the contemporary indifference to handling of accidentals would make the extensive revision appear to him wasteful. However, another explanation exists. If we grant that the printer's copy resembled my manuscript in its handling of sentences ending within the line, and if we further grant that a compositor might rather faithfully follow clearly written copy, then the proof-sheets might resemble the manuscript, with end punctuation and lower case. But a proofreader might object; he would revise eight of the nine in I i, but on seeing how numerous this kind of error is, he might not want to make the extra work for the compositor of justifying (re-spacing) again every line that had a lower case letter replaced by a wider upper case letter. The easiest way to circumvent the problem would be to replace the final punctuation with another kind of punctuation, thus lessening the labor of the printer in correcting proof. Finally, the evidence of the 48 lines in which 1639 follows the manuscript does not bear much weight, because many Elizabethan texts do not capitalize the first letter of the word following a rhetorical question or exclamation. Of these 48 lines, 35 have a question mark followed by a lower case letter, 2 have an exclamation point followed by a lower case letter, and 11 have final punctuation followed by a proper noun.

While the differences in mid-line punctuation and capitalization of sentences ending within a speech provide considerable reason for believing that the printer's copy closely resembled my manuscript, further reason is found in the compositor's misreading of the passage at III ii 50-53. His errors are described in detail in Appendix 4, but his confusion about line 53 is especially illuminating. The manuscript appears thus:

      Caes: giue me the letter; I'll peruse it now.
                              'reades'

      Agrippa.   Agri: Cæsar!
      Caes: here the woman writes   III ii 52-53

The 1639 edition attributes line 52 to Agrippa, omitting both line 51 spoken by Plancus and the speech prefix "Caes:" of line 52. Thus Caesar's command for the letter and all of line 52, including the stage direction, is given to Agrippa. The compositor now had to set the first three words of line 53. If his copy looked like the transcription above, but with the additional stage direction "They retire" written as a revision by the author in the right margin after the three names, a stage direction appearing in 1639, he could easily have misinterpreted Caesar's call to Agrippa, the speech prefix "Agri:" and Agrippa's acknowledgement of Caesar's call as a stage direction naming the three men who were to "retire." He did not understand that Agrippa and Agri. were the same person, and he did not understand the relationship between the list of names and the stage direction. This explanation of the compositor's error in setting the three names in upper case roman as a stage direction is thus easily explained by supposing that his copy divided line 53 as it is divided in the manuscript. If the last half of line 53 had been written on the same line as the first half, the compositor could hardly have made the error he did.

The Substantive Changes in 1639 Are Generally Authorial

The argument so far has tried to show first, that the substantive revisions in the manuscript are authorial, second, that the manuscript precedes the printed play in date, and third, that the printed play depends for its source on a manuscript nearly identical

in appearance to mine. If the printing house copy was nearly identical
the question then arises if the revisions appearing in the printed
copy are authorial or not. My argument for the second point
listed above, that the manuscript precedes the printed play in
date, also provides the examples for believing that the revisions
of the manuscript appearing in the 1639 edition are probably
authorial. The kind of revision seen in the minor changes
made in the manuscript is the same kind of revision made in
1639. The tendency of both sets of revisions is to change relatively
few passages, to not thoroughly overhaul speeches or passages
but to make minor corrections, and to show concern for the
particular word rather than the broad effect. If the examples
adduced for the second point show that the 1639 revisions generally
make minor improvements in expression that are of a piece with
the rest of the play, and if the tendency of the revisions of
both manuscript and 1639 is alike, then the revisions for 1639
were probably made by the author in his copy for the printer.

The Manuscript Subjected to Styling of Accidentals

However, the author's carefully prepared manuscript was
unfortunately subjected to compositorial styling of its pointing.
In her edition of the play, Sister Mary claims that the 1639
edition shows a very careful attention to the accidentals of the
text. I do not believe her. The differences in punctuation
between the manuscript and the 1639 edition listed in copious
detail in Appendix 3, the historical collation, show that the

author's intentions in this matter were not carried out. The
differences also show that the 1639 edition frequently punctuates
erratically and sometimes senselessly. For example, in the
manuscript Cleopatra says

> Hail mighty Prince; for that high name the Godds
> Whoo reft mee of it, have bestow'd on thee.
> V iii 20-21

The 1639 edition replaces the comma with a question mark.[70]
Generally, 1639 uses heavier pointing that the manuscript, replacing
manuscript commas with semi-colons, semi-colons with colons, and
inserting punctuation where none exists and none is needed. The
spelling of 1639 is much more modern than the spelling of the
manuscript. The printed copy uses "u-v" and "i-j" in the modern
way while the manuscript retains them as complements, it
generally drops the extra letter at the end of such manuscript
words as "thinke," "Queene," "whoo," and "yett," and it
modernizes the regular manuscript "ei" in "feilds" or "yeild"
to "fields" and "yield," modernizes "howers" to "houres," but
prefers "bloud" to "blood." The printed play is not as consistent in its spelling practice as the manuscript. Since orthography
was unsettled at the time of this play, the great number of
differences in spelling between manuscript and 1639 only show
that the spelling of the printer's copy was subjected to compositorial styling as was the punctuation. The regular practice of
the period leads one to expect it.

The Text Must Be Established
by a Conflation

I have attempted to show that the manuscript rather than the
1639 edition ought to be regarded as the copy-text. My belief
is that the copy from which the one compositor set the 1639
edition was in the same hand as the manuscript. Surely practices
of punctuation and capitalization varied from scribe to scribe
as much as they did from printing house to printing house,
and the evidence offered about the copy-text shows that certain
passages and details in the 1639 edition can best be explained
by the compositor having looked at copy nearly identical to the
manuscript. Certain substantive revisions appearing in 1639,
however, were made in the printer's copy, and the character of
many of these revisions suggests that they were made by the
reviser of the manuscript, who, we have both external and internal
evidence to believe, was the author. Those revisions that
seem to be authorial, therefore, must be included in the text.
But because the accidentals of the printed play show the practice
of proofreader and compositor, the accidentals of the manuscript
more accurately represent the author's practice. An adequate
text must therefore be an eclectic text, presenting the accidentals and old-spelling texture of the manuscript, but incorporating
in it the substantive authorial revisions made in the 1639
edition (without subjecting those revisions to normalization).
The text I have established therefore, is a conflation of the
manuscript and the 1639 edition.

4. The Treatment of the Copy-Text

The collation of the manuscript and 1639 edition was made from microfilms and Xerox reproductions of the microfilm. These reproductions are generally satisfactory for producing an edition, but they have certain shortcomings. For example, one cannot tell from either Xerox or microfilm of 1639 if a black dot following the last word in a line but superior to the ordinary position for a period is a turned letter or a flaw in the paper. Or again, one could not establish from either microfilm or a Xerox reproduction of 1639 whether the play was printed as a duodecimo (as it in fact was) or as a quarto gathered in sixes because no water marks or chain lines are visible on the paper.

I made a word-by-word, point-by-point comparison of the printed copies against the control text of the manuscript, which I typed on cards, one line per card. I chose the manuscript as the control text because a reading of the manuscript and a printed copy showed in the manuscript a number of presumably authorial revisions as well as an exactness in pointing, while the printed copy showed many irregularities, especially in pointing. The copies of 1639 were collated against the cards, and every variation was recorded that could possibly have significance, including differences in spelling, capitalization, and pointing. I took no notice in the collation of wrong-fount letters in the 1639 edition, of display capitals, of variable spacing, or of other mechanical features of the typesetting (such as an unjustified em-space, for example). I established the text by a line-by-line comparison of the recorded variants, generally retaining the punctuation and spelling of the copy-text, but incorporating in it what appear to be authorial revisions in the 1639 edition.

In a recent essay, Bowers suggests that a collation of five or six copies ought to give an editor a fair idea of whether any great differences because of press correction are going to occur or not.[71] Since my collation of five printed copies shows that they offer no extensive alternate readings, no substantive differences in even single words, and only twelve spelling variants, I have not felt it necessary to collate all the known copies. In her edition of the play, Sister Mary collated the Harvard, Yale, Huntington, University of Chicago, and Pforzheimer copies, the last two of which I have not collated, and found no significant variations. My choice of the five copies was made arbitrarily; I asked the large libraries that would most likely have microfilming facilities to make a copy. I had intended to collate six copies, but the Library of Congress reported that its copy was too brittle to microfilm.

The collation of copy-text and printed copies showed that emendation of accidentals and lineation had to be made. A list of accidentals altered from the copy-text appears as Appendix 1. The alterations have been kept to a minimum. Obvious errors in punctuation have been corrected, and spelling differing from the ordinary spelling of the manuscript has been altered. In only four instances are the emendations mine; the others are made from the 1639 edition. I have once emended a misspelled word incorporated in the copy-text from 1639 (at V iii 73). The lines are not numbered in either the manuscript or 1639. Using the scene as the unit, I have numbered the lines of the text, but not numbered the act and scene headings or the stage directions. When lines were added to the copy-text from the authorial revisions appearing in 1639, the numbering of the lines in the copy-text was changed so that the added lines are numbered in sequence.

The accidentals of the copy-text have been generally retained, except for the silent alterations described below. Eccentricities of spelling have been retained, except in the case of obvious error (such as "matclesse" for "matchlesse") when the alteration is described in Appendix 1. Punctuation is little altered; except for the relatively few instances when one of the silent alterations is made, the change is listed in appendix 1. The capitalization of the copy-text has been much more extensively altered than either spelling or punctuation, and the changes are described in the section on silent alterations below. The infrequent occurrence of a capital letter as the first letter of a word other than a proper noun occurring within the sentence has been retained. I have attempted to retain the general texture of the accidentals of the copy-text without retaining features that unnecessarily prove to be stumbling blocks for a modern reader (such as the "u-v" complements or the lack of a capital letter as the first letter of a word beginning a sentence).

The few press-variants that were discovered are recorded in Appendix 2. They are not of sufficient number or of a nature to be useful in identifying the sophistication of text characteristic of either printing house or compositor. Most appear to be simple spelling corrections made on already proofed sheets or the correction of a missing letter made on the press after several sheets had been printed and the omission noticed. The piece of type could have been dropped from the chase while the lock-up was being moved from stone to press either before or after proofing.[72]

Both manuscript and 1639 divide the play into five acts at similar places, but neither divides the acts into scenes. I have divided the play into scenes in order to aid the reader who is accustomed to scene headings to make the transition from one scene to the next. May ordinarily ends a scene with the exit of all the characters and the appearance of new ones or a change of location, so the task of making a division into scenes is not difficult. I have also made a scene division when important characters remain on stage after the exit of others and take up a new topic for discussion, but I have not followed the strict neo-classic practice of making a scene division for the entry or exit of every character, no matter how minor.

5. Silent Alterations

Bowers seems to me correct in asserting in his essay on the text of his edition of Dekker's <u>Dramatic</u> <u>Works</u> that

> a critical edition is neither a diplomatic nor a facsimile reprint addressed principally to those who need to make a close study of the most minute formal characteristics of a text, and hence some degree of silent alteration is advisable.[73]

The silent alterations I have made are not substantive or semi-substantive, but chiefly concern capitalization, italicization, punctuation, indention, and certain orthographical conventions.

First, lower case letters which are normally used in the manuscript
as the first letter of the first word of an address following a
speech prefix (unless that first word is the first person pronoun
or a proper noun, when an upper case letter is used as the first
letter), the normal form of the manuscript, are silently raised
to upper case. Since 1639 prints speech prefixes centered above
the line, the first letter of the first word in the first line
of the speech is capitalized in accordance with the convention
of capitalizing the first letter in any line of verse. In the
manuscript, however, the speech prefix is written on the same line
as the first line of the speech, and the copyist ordinarily does not
capitalize the first letter. Also, lower case letters at the
beginning of a sentence following a full stop within a speech, the
normal form of the manuscript, are silently raised to upper case
in the text, the footnotes, and all appendices except Appendix 5,
which lists accidentals and variants in the 1639 printed copies'
handling of sentences ending within the line in the manuscript.
I have also raised to upper case the lower case first letter of
a word beginning a clause after a question or exclamation
mark. Second, names of persons, which are italicized in
1639 but are not italicized in the manuscript, are silently
italicized in the text, the footnotes, and all appendices except
Appendix 5. In spite of the fact that the italicizing of both
names of persons and places was "the usual practice in carefully
printed dramatic texts of the time,"[74] I have not italicized place
names because the manuscript does not do so, and 1639 does so
erratically, only irregularly conforming to the custom of italicizing

the names of cities and countries. I have silently italicized
the song at I ii 58-69, since it is italicized in 1639 in accord
with current practice. Third, some punctuation has been silently
altered. The manuscript's regular use of a colon at the end of
a speech prefix has been normalized to a period. Faulty or missing
punctuation in a series of names or at the end of a stage direction
has been silently emended. I have, however, recorded any alteration
made in the end punctuation of a speech in Appendices 1 and 3, the
list of accidentals altered from the copy-text and the collation of
the manuscript and 1639. Fourth, a part-line which completes a
preceding line of verse is indented since the practice has been
"traditional for dramatic texts since Capell."[75] The practice
of the manuscript varies in this matter, since sometimes one
line of the manuscript contains a speech prefix, a half-line,
another speech prefix, and the remaining half-line, while
at other times the speech prefixes and half-lines will appear on
successive lines of the manuscript, but the second half-line will
not be indented. The variable practice caused some temporary
confusion while I was numbering the lines, but May's regular five
stresses enabled me to number correctly. Fifth, certain orthographical conventions in both manuscript and print have been dealt with
consistently. The manuscript regularly uses long "s" and the "u-v,"
"i-j" complements. These have been modernized, since Bowers per-
suasively argues that their presence needlessly places stumbling
blocks in the path of a general reader in an old-spelling edition and
that their modernization causes no linguistic anomalies.[76] Further,
the 1639 edition retains the long "s" initially and medially, as
was the custom of English printers until about 1800,[77] but ordinarily

modernizes the "u-v," "i-j" complements. The manuscript also occasionally writes a superscript "e" in "Mai^{e}sty" (as at I i 38); I have silently normalized it. Ligatures peculiar to the copy-text have been retained, such as "œ" in "Cœlosyria" (which was retained by 1639) and "æ" in "æqualize" (which was not). I have also retained the copy-text "ȝ" and "ȣ".

When lines, part-lines, or words have been incorporated into the text, my practice has been to retain the spelling, punctuation, and capitalization of the printed copy rather than to normalize it to conform to the usual practice of the manuscript. In lines, part-lines, and words included from 1639, I have raised to upper case the lower case first letter of the first word after a full stop within an address, modernized long "s", and indented part-lines beginning an address. Since the printed copies are not used as the copy-text, my ignoring of certain typographical features in those collated seems justified. I have not recorded such mechanical features as running heads, ornaments, catch-words, signatures, display capitals, the upper case letter following a display capital, turned letters, wrong fount, misspacing, indistinct letters, ligatures, such as "ct" and "st", or obvious misspellings. When turned letters, misspacing, or obvious printer's errors (such as "thi?" for "this" at IV i 202) occur in passages from the 1639 edition incorporated in the text, they are silently corrected.

The paraphernalia, such as scene headings and stage directions, have been silently emended in certain ways. Act headings, present in both manuscript and 1639, are included, but missing end punctuation is silently supplied and capitalization silently made consistent.

Scene headings, supplied by me, are enclosed in brackets. Speech headings are variously abbreviated in both manuscript and 1639; I have made them consistent, choosing the form in which they most often appear in the copy-text. If speech headings are supplied by me, they are bracketed. In accordance with the practice of the 1639 edition and other Elizabethan dramatic texts, I have italicized all speech headings. None were italicized in the copy-text. The dorm of stage directions has been changed from that of the copy-text to that of the 1639 edition and other Elizabethan dramatic texts. Names appear in Roman type, the rest in italics. The manuscript made no distinction. The 1639 edition used upper case Roman for all letters in names, but I have followed the manuscript and used upper case in only the first letter of a name. Names variously abbreviated in stage directions in the copy-text are silently made consistent with the form of the abbreviation in the speech prefixes. Names abbreviated in entrance directions in the copy-text are silently expanded for consistency. The first letter of the first word of a stage direction is silently raised to upper case if it is in lower case. End punctuation is silently supplied for stage directions if missing, or made into a full point if it appears as a suspension. If the stage direction is supplied by me, it is bracketed. Entrances are silently centered, and exits are set in the right hand margin. Brief stage directions are set in the right hand margin. Marginal notes have been dealt with consistently. All are set in italics, in accord with 1639 but of course not in accord with the manuscript, and the variable practice of ending abbreviations with either a colon or a period in the manuscript has been regularized to a period. I have positioned the marginal notes as they were in the copy-text.

When speech headings are incorporated in the copy-text from the 1639 edition, they are made consistent in spelling, placed at the left of the line rather than centered above it as in 1639, and all letters except the first are reduced to lower case, since they are printed in upper case in 1639.

6. The Apparatus of the Text

The apparatus of this edition is intended to serve a threefold purpose. It is intended to provide the reader first with all the facts necessary to reconstruct the significant details of the copy text, and second with all the facts from which the text was established.[78] In order to reconstruct the copy-text, a reader may consult the footnotes, Appendix 1 (the list of accidentals altered from the copy-text), and the description of the classes of silent alterations in part four of this textual introduction. In order to possess all the facts from which the text was made, a reader may consult Appendix 2 (a list of press-variant formes of the 1639 edition), Appendix 3 (a collation of the manuscript and five copies of the 1639 edition), Appendix 5 (a list of accidentals and variants in the 1639 printed copies' handling of sentences ending within the line in the manuscript), and the description of silent alterations. The third purpose of the apparatus is to explain difficult or obscure textual or critical problems. Appendices 4 and 6 provide explanatory textual notes and explanatory

critical notes respectively. In footnotes and appendices I have
used two of McKerrow's shorthand symbols.[79] The inferior caret
in collations of punctuation indicates the absence of pointing in
either the copy-text or the 1639 edition (name!] ~_∧ 1639),
and the wavy dash in collations of punctuation takes the place
of the preceding word which locates the pointing. Elision is
indicated by three dots. Brief explanations of the form of each
appendix are prefixed to the appendix when necessary.

The footnotes to the text list only substantive departures from
the copy-text. In accordance with Bowers' suggestions and practice,[80]
I have listed this class of information alone on the page of the
text itself, choosing in this way to call to the reader's attention
important variants in the substance of the text. Addison, in
Spectator No. 470, has the truth of it when he says

> indeed, when a different reading gives us a
> different sense, or a new elegance in an author,
> the editor does very well in taking notice of
> it; but when he only entertains us with the several
> ways of spelling the same word, and gathers
> together the various blunders and mistakes of
> twenty or thirty different transcribers, they only
> take up the time of the learned reader, and
> puzzle the minds of the ignorant.[81]

Appendix 1 lists the accidentals altered from the copy-text.
I have put this class of information in a separate appendix so as
not to "take up the time of the learned reader" with non-substantive
matter in the footnotes, and second, to make easily accessible
the non-substantive facts necessary to reconstruct the copy-text.
Silent alterations are not included in the list. The relatively
few altered accidentals bear witness to the clean copy and careful
revision of the manuscript. In one trivial matter the list in

Appendix 1 errs. For example, at II i 99 in Appendix 1 I write "countrey.] 1639;∧ms." The intention of the entry is to call attention to the insertion in the text of a full stop missing in the copy-text but found in all copies of the 1639 edition. However, in order to describe the position of the full stop in the line, I had to write the word preceding the stop, and the entry suggests that "countrey," spelled so, is also found in 1639. It is not; the word is there spelled "Country." Since I have not recorded spelling differences in the historical collation, it is only sensible not to record them here, and to allow the variant spelling of 1639 to be overlooked.

Appendix 2 lists the press-variant formes of the 1639 edition, by sheet, inner and outer forme. The variants are few in number, non-substantive, and generally comprise correction of obvious misspellings. Since no variant substantive readings appear, the list is of course not useful in establishing the authority of readings on purely physical evidence. Several inferences can safely be made, however. The relatively few non-substantive readings show that the author made no corrections of his play once printing got under way, that the compositor, therefore, worded from a manuscript rather carefully prepared for the printer, and, given the Elizabethan compositor's freedom in spelling and pointing, that the proofreading and proof correction were accomplished before these corrections were made. Of the nine variants, three might be caused by worn or unjustified type. For example, the Huntington copy has the word "time," Yale has "tim" and Folger has "time" with the "e" making only a faint impression

(II i 117). If these three variants are included, then six of the variants show a letter missing and replaced, two show one letter substituted for another, and one shows a garbled spelling corrected. Such sparse correction suggests that none of the sheets in the copies collated is uncorrected in the true sense of representing a sheet pulled from the press before the proofreader had read it and the compositor corrected it. The existence of such truly uncorrected sheets is easily accounted for by the customary procedure of Elizabethan printers while printing with two skeletons,[82] and the insertion of letters inadvertently dropped from the chase is commonplace in printing shops even today. I think that the sheets in the copies I collated were proofread and corrected, and the variants listed in Appendix 2 represent further correction.

Appendix 3 is a collation of the substantive and semi-substantive variants from the manuscript and the 1639 edition. The collation is keyed to the present edited text and not to the copy-text. The appendix contains all the rejected manuscript readings that are listed in the footnotes, all rejected 1639 substantive readings, all rejected 1639 punctuation, all rejected copy-text punctuation, and differences in elided words, since they are of metrical importance. I have taken no notice in the collation of spelling in the 1639 edition differing from the spelling of the manuscript, since the spelling of Elizabethan compositors is notably idiosyncratic. Therefore no notice is taken of spelling differences in such a notation as that for (III i 85), "yeilding]∧~,

1639," whereas the printed copy in fact spells "yielding." The
compositor of this edition was in certain matters "modern." He
modernized the "u-v" "i-j" complements ("love" for the manuscript
"loue"), usually dropped final "e" ("aloof" for the manuscript
"aloofe"), and so preferred "esteems" to manuscript "esteemes"
and "eys" to "eyes." I have also not listed upper case letters
as the first letter in a word within the sentence in 1639 but
lower case in the manuscript, not listed lower case letters as
the first letter in a word within the sentence in 1639 but upper
case in the manuscript, not listed nouns italicized in 1639 but
not in the manuscript (as <u>Chaos</u> II iv 6), nor listed place names
occasionally italicized in 1639 (<u>Cyprus</u>) but never italicized
in the manuscript.

Appendix 4 contains the explanatory textual notes, in
which I discuss all important emendations or refusals to emend.
I have not discussed every substantive emendation of the copy-
text, since many of the one or two word revisions in 1639 seem
little better than the original of the copy-text. Few of the
revisions are longer than two lines, and few of the revisions
of any length seem to me to be great improvements, although the
purpose of most of them is easily discernible. May was simply
not a great writer.

In accepting or rejecting variant readings, I have found
that considerable difficulty arises in separating minor substantive
authorial revision from authoritative texts, Greg favoring the
reading of the copy-text and Bowers the reading of the revised
edition. Greg says,

> suppose that the claims of two readings, one in
> the copy-text and one in some other authority
> appear to be exactly balanced; what then should
> an editor do? In such a case, while there can
> be no logical reason for giving preference to the
> copy-text, in practice, if there is no reason for
> altering its reading, the obvious thing seems to
> be to let it stand.[83]

Greg also offers three rules to govern the choice of variants if more than one substantive text exists. First,

> the opinion the editor may form respecting
> the nature of the copy from which each sub-
> stantive edition was printed, which is a matter
> of external authority,[84]

governs the choice of variants. Second, Greg says, choose variants

> partly by the intrinsic authority of the several
> texts as judged by the relative frequency of
> manifest errors therein.[85]

As shown by the footnotes and Appendix 1, accidentals changed in the copy-text, the manuscript is remarkably free of errors in spelling, punctuation, and sense, and the 1639 edition contains frequent errors of these classes. The manuscript ought to be authoritative in indifferent cases. Third, variants in substantive editions should be chosen

> partly by the judgement of the intrinsic claims
> of individual readings to orginality.[86]

This rule enables the editor to weigh the merits of each variant, choosing those that, because they are manifestly superior, show a reason for being made, or are similar to revisions made by the author in the manuscript, ought to be incorporated in the text.

In his most recent statement about the choice of variants,

Bowers says that

> if the variation seems much of a piece, the odds favor the general acceptance of all the substantive readings of the revised edition save for manifest or strongly suspected error. That is, verbal variants in the revision are to be taken as innocent until proved guilty as printer's errors.[87]

Greg's views on the choice of variants were written in 1942 before he had developed a clear rationale of copy-text, and his conservative views support a close adherence to the copy-text, an adherence he repudiated in 1950 when he referred to the "tyranny of the copy-text."[88] Yet Bowers' more recent view enjoins an equally rigid acceptance of substantives from one text unless bibliographical evidence can ascertain that the compositor has erred. The difference, of course, is in Bowers' faith in bibliographical techniques when used to determine the authority of variant readings, and Greg's reliance on the copy-text because techniques to determine authority did not exist.

Neither Greg's nor Bowers' view can be singly used to fix the principle to choose variants in this edition of Cleopatra. Since Cleopatra exists in manuscript and printed edition, Greg's first rule does not hold, his second rule is more suitably applied to what he later recognized as accidentals rather than substantives, and his third rule tends toward personal predilection. On the other hand, to "prove" a variant a printer's error as Bowers asks is a difficult task when the press-variant formes are as few as in this edition. Had the compositor erred, and one of the uncorrected sheets found its way into a finished copy (a not unusual procedure when printing with two skeletons in the normal fashion[89]), and then had the forme been corrected and printing continued so a corrected state appeared in a copy, proof for a printer's error would be air tight. But surely one should "strongly suspect" such 1639 variants as "ruine" for copy-text "ruines" (I i 55), "stor'd" for copy-text "stirr'd" (II iv 105), "better think" for copy-text "thinke better" (III iii 37), and "hence" for copy-text "thence" (IV i 68), each of which represents a class of errors easily attributed to a compositor. Such errors, which in context do make sense, are even more suspect when errors of the same class occur which do not make sense in the context, as 1639 "teem'd" for copy-text "seem'd" (I i 66), and "vexes" for copy-text "wexes" (I ii 37). Generally I have chosen to follow Bowers in the choice of variant readings, preferring the substantive revisions of 1639. However, when I "strongly suspect" an error of the kind described above, I prefer the copy-text reading to that of 1639.

Appendix 5 is a list of accidentals and variants in the 1634 edition's handling of sentences ending within the line within an address in the manuscript. In this appendix only have I indicated differences in copy-text and 1639 italicization, spelling, capitalization, and punctuation. I have, however, modernized long "s" and the "u-v" "i-j" complements for ease of reading.

Appendix 6 contains the explanatory critical notes. Most of them define recondite words or offer historical information about the classical age. The play contains few passages in which the sense is not clear at once or may easily be discerned, but where ambiguity is present, I have offered an explanation. I have found no specific topical allusions, but the lack of allusion need not be unexpected in a play written on a classical subject by a man as immersed in the classical period as Thomas May.

Footnotes

[1]George F. Warner and Julius P. Gilson, A Catalogue of Western Manuscripts in the Old Royal and King's Collections, 4 vols. (London, 1921), II, 302.

[2]A full study of May's poem was done by R. T. Bruère, "The Latin and English Versions of Thomas May's Supplementum Lucani," Classical Philology, XLIV (1949), 145-163.

[3]Warner and Gilson, II, 302.

[4]W. W. Greg, A Bibliography of English Printed Drama to the Restoration, 4 vols. (London, 1939-1959), II, 693.

[5]Alfred Harbage, Annals of English Drama, 975-1700 (Philadelphia, 1940), pp. 98-99.

[6]Sister Mary Ransom Burke, The Tragedy of Cleopatra, Queene of Ægypt, Edited, with an Introduction (Fordham, 1943).

[7]Thomas Bladon, "Thomas May's Tragedy of Agrippina," Notes and Queries, 4th series, II (1868), 132; Allan G. Chester, Thomas May: Man of Letters 1595-1650 (Philadelphia, 1932), p. 189; Greg, A Bibliography, II, 693.

[8]The Library of Congress National Union Catalogue located at Washington, D.C.

[9]Greg, A Bibliography, II, 693.

[10]A.W. Pollard and G.R. Redgrave, A Short-title Catalogue of Books Printed in England, Scotland, and Ireland and of English Books Printed Abroad 1475-1640 (London, 1926), p. 401.

[11]Sister Mary, p. cv.

[12]Ibid., p. xciii.

[13]Heinrich Wolfe, Thomas May's Tragedy of Cleopatra, Queen of Ægypt (Strassburg, 1914).

[14]Bernard M. Wagner, "Manuscript Plays of the Seventeenth Century," Times Literary Supplement, October 4, 1934, p. 675.

[15]Sister M. Simplicia Fitzgibbons, ed., Thomas May The Old Couple (Washington, D.C., 1943).

[16]Alexander Werner, Thomas May als Lustspieldichter (1894).

[17] F.E. Schmid, ed., *The Tragedy of Julia Agrippina, Empresse of Rome*, in W. Bang, ed., *Materialen zur Kunde des Älteren Englischen Dramas*, XLIII (Louvain, 1914).

[18] Allan G. Chester, *Thomas May: Man of Letters 1595-1650* (Philadelphia, 1932).

[19] G.E. Bentley, *The Jacobean and Caroline Stage*, 5 vols. (Oxford, 1941-1956), IV, 830-841.

[20] W.D. Briggs, "The Influence of Jonson's Tragedy in the Seventeenth Century," *Anglia*, XXXV (1912), 277-337.

[21] R.B. McKerrow, *The Works of Thomas Nashe*, 5 vols. (London, 1904-1910).

[22] F. S. Boas, *The Works of Thomas Kyd* (Oxford, 1901).

[23] McKerrow, *Nashe*, I, xi-xvi.

[24] For amusing and shocking examples of the high-handed procedures of early and even modern editors, see Fredson Bowers, *Textual and Literary Criticism* (Cambridge, England, 1958), pp. 4-5, 9, 24-26.

[25] See F. Bowers, "Current Theories of Copy-text, with an Illustration from Dryden," *Modern Philology*, XLVIII (1950), 12.

[26] Ibid.

[27] F. Bowers, "Established Texts and Definitive Editions," *Philological Quarterly*, XLI (1962), 9-10.

[28] Bowers, "Current Theories," 12.

[29] See W. W. Greg, *The Editorial Problem in Shakespeare* (Oxford, 1942), p. x, and R.B. McKerrow, *Prolegomena for the Oxford Shakespeare* (Oxford, 1939), p. 6.

[30] R. B. McKerrow, *Prolegomena*.

[31] Ibid., pp. 6, 14.

[32] Bowers, "Current Theories," 12; see McKerrow, *Prolegomena*, pp. 17-18.

[33] McKerrow, *Prolegomena*, pp. 13-14; Greg, *Editorial Problems* pp. xxii, xxvi.

[34] Greg, *Editorial Problems*.

[35] Ibid., p. xxviii.

[36] McKerrow, *Prolegomena*, p. 8.

[37] Greg, *Editorial Problems*, p. xxxvii.

[38] *Ibid.*, p. xxxvi.

[39] *Ibid.*

[40] Bowers, "Current Theories," 13.

[41] *Ibid.*

[42] Greg, *Editorial Problems*, p. xxxvi; McKerrow, *Prolegomena*, p. 18.

[43] Greg, *Editorial Problems*, pp. xxvii-xxix.

[44] See, for example, F. Bowers, "Notes on Running Titles as Bibliographical Evidence," *The Library*, 4th series, XIX (1938), 315-338; W. W. Greg, *The Variants in the First Quarto of King Lear: A Bibliographical and Critical Inquiry* (London, 1940); and Charlton Hinman, "Principles Governing the Use of Variant Spellings as Evidence of Alternate Setting by Two Compositors," *The Library*, 4th series, XXI (1940), 78-94.

[45] W. W. Greg, "The Rationale of Copy-text," *Studies in Bibliography*, III (1950), 19-36.

[46] *Ibid.*, 19-20.

[47] McKerrow, *Prolegomena*, pp. 17-18.

[48] See Bowers, "Established Texts."

[49] *Ibid.*, 13.

[50] *Ibid.*

[51] F. Bowers, *On Editing Shakespeare* (Philadelphia, 1955), p. 119, n. 19. Bowers describes other classes of textual problems solved in *Hamlet* by compositor analysis on pp. 38-46 and pp. 74-75.

[52] Bowers, *Textual and Literary Criticism*, pp. 120-121.

[53] *Ibid.*, p. 122.

[54] *Ibid.*

[55] "Rules for the Guidance of Editors of the Society's Reprints," in *Collections* I, 2, *The Malone Society* (Oxford, 1908), 113-116, and *Collections* IV, *The Malone Society* (Oxford, 1956), 66-69.

[56] Edward J. Howard, ed., *Of the Knowledge Which Maketh a Wise Man*, by Sir Thomas Elyot (Oxford, Ohio, 1946).

[57] Thomas M. Cranfill, ed., *Rich's Farewell to Military Profession 1581*, by Barnabe Rich (Austin, Texas, 1959).

[58] See John Russell Brown, "The Rationale of Old-Spelling Editions of the Plays of Shakespeare and his Contemporaries," *Studies in Bibliography*, XIII (1960), 49-68, and Arthur Brown, "The Rationale of Old-Spelling Editions of the Plays of Shakespeare and his Contemporaries: A Rejoinder," *Studies in Bibliography*, XIII (1960), 69-76.

[59] Bowers, *Textual and Literary Criticism*, p. 123.

[60] Ibid., p. 125.

[61] Ibid.

[62] Greg, *Editorial Problems*, p. xx.

[63] He is not included in W. W. Greg, ed., *English Literary Autographs 1550-1650*, 3 vols. and suppl. (Oxford, 1925-1932).

[64] Warner and Gilson, II, 303.

[65] Ibid., p. 302.

[66] Sister Mary, pp. cxiv-cxxiv.

[67] W. W. Greg, "An Elizabethan Printer and His Copy," *The Library*, 4th series, IV (1924), 108.

[68] Bowers, "Established Texts," 9.

[69] Ibid., 8.

[70] Further examples occur at I ii 169, IV i 67, V iii 25, and throughout.

[71] F. Bowers, "Textual Criticism," in James Thorpe, ed., *The Aims and Methods of Scholarship in Modern Languages and Literatures* (New York, 1963), p. 33, n. 20.

[72] For a description of Elizabethan proofing with one and two skeletons, see F. Bowers, "Elizabethan Proofing," in James G. McManaway, et al., eds., *Joseph Quincy Adams Memorial Studies* (Washington, D.C., 1948), pp. 571-586, and n. 1-3, p. 571, listing other articles on proofing.

[73] F. Bowers, "The Text of This Edition," in *The Dramatic Works of Thomas Dekker*, 4 vols. (Cambridge, England, 1953-1961), I, xii.

[74] Ibid., p. xiii.

[75] Ibid.

[76] F. Bowers, "Old-Spelling Editions of Dramatic Texts," in Don Cameron Allen, ed., *Studies in Honor of T.W. Baldwin* (Urbana Illinois, 1958), p. 14, and Bowers, *Textual and Literary Criticism*, p. 148.

[77] R. B. McKerrow, *An Introduction to Bibliography* (Oxford, 1928), p. 309.

[78] Such is the function of the apparatus as described by Bowers, "Textual Criticism," in *The Aims and Methods of Scholarship*, p. 41.

[79] McKerrow, *Prolegomena*, pp. 86-97.

[80] Bowers, *Textual and Literary Criticism*, p. 124, and Bowers, *Dekker*.

[81] Quoted in Bowers, *Dekker*, I, x, n. 1.

[82] Bowers, "Elizabethan Proofing," pp. 571-586.

[83] Greg, "Rationale," 31.

[84] Ibid., 29.

[85] Ibid.

[86] Ibid.

[87] Bowers, "Textual Criticism," in *The Aims and Methods of Scholarship*, p. 31.

[88] Greg, "Rationale," 26.

[89] See Bowers, "Elizabethan Proofing," pp. 571-586.

While no measure of greatness can be claimed for May's Cleopatra, neither does it entirely deserve Furness's condemnation as the "weakest and least imaginative" of all versions of the Cleopatra story.[1] If to be weak and unimaginative is to be highly dependent on one's great contemporaries and to reveal the new tendencies in the thought of one's age, there is ground for Furness's opinion; but, in my view, his play may be more accurately described as a derivative and competent version which reveals a new skeptical spirit, "the sophisticated, satirical, conflicting mood, deeply divided, of the Jacobean drama."[2] Its inadequacies in style and its inconsistencies of characterization show clearly when it is compared to Shakespeare's Antony and Cleopatra, but to describe its inferiority is not to point out its significant features. For May, in defiance of the long-established traditional interpretation of Cleopatra's character, makes her unfaithful to Antony and unscrupulous in her use of him to achieve her selfish ends.

The traditional interpretation of Cleopatra's character in the centuries preceding May's version establishes her loyalty to Antony. Boccaccio, Chaucer, Gower, Lydgate, and sisteenth-century dramatists both English and Continental established the tradition of her loyalty.

Boccaccio shows Cleopatra loyal in De Casibus Illustrium Virorum, as Lydgate's "embroider[ed]" translation of the French version[3] makes clear. Her avarice and pride were so great,

Lydgate says, that, to please her and make her empress, Antony began the war on Octavius. But she is not a schemer, and upon Antony's death she is inconsolable:

> Of whos deth the queen Cleopatras
> Took a sorwe verry importable;
> Because ther was no recure in the caas,
> Thouhte of his wo she wolde be partable,
> Whos fatal eende pitous & lamentable:
> Slouh eek hirsilf, loue so did hir raue;
> Afftir thei bothe buryed in o graue.[4]

Boccaccio tells Cleopatra's story at greater length in De Claris Mulieribus, showing a greedy, lustful, pleasure-seeking queen with an "insatiable . . . craving for kingdoms"[5] who is loyal to Antony while he lives except for one lapse. She and Antony are pleasure-loving sensualists, and, while Boccaccio does not say they do not love each other, neither does he say they do. We can only infer that she loves him for what he can give her because she has been a self-seeker all her life. When Cleopatra first acquired Egypt "through two crimes" she

> gave herself to her pleasures, Having become
> almost the prostitute of Oriental kings, and
> greedy for gold and jewels, she not only stripped
> her lovers of these things with her art, but it
> is said that she emptied the sacred places of the
> Egyptians of their vases, statues, and other treasures.[6]

She greedily accepts Antony's gifts of parts of Syria and
Arabia, and of Artabasdes, the captive king with all his booty.[7]
While Antony was in Parthia, her greed nearly caused her to be
unfaithful, because she

> sent messengers to [Herod Antipater] to
> bring him to her embraces, so that, if he
> accepted, she could take as payment the
> kingdom he had gained shortly before through
> Antony.[8]

But Herod refused her offer "through respect for Antony."[9]
She finally asked Antony for the Roman Empire itself, and Antony,

> without properly considering his own strength
> or the power of the Romans, promised to give it
> to her, as if it were his to give.[10]

Boccaccio thus emphasizes her craving for wealth rather than
any other characteristic. Except for the incident with Herod,
she remains loyal to Antony until his death.

Chaucer follows Boccaccio and makes Cleopatra one of love's
martyrs in his <u>Legend of Good Women</u>, thus helping establish the
tradition of her loyalty. Robinson, Chaucer's learned editor,
says that

> there can be no doubt that in the mind of
> Chaucer and his contemporaries the heroines he cele-
> brates were good in the only sense that counted
> for the purpose in hand--they were faithful followers
> of the god of Love.[11]

Chaucer does not describe in detail Antony's and Cleopatra's life before Antony's death, but after Antony's suicide, Chaucer says that Cleopatra had a "shrine" made of precious jewels, filled with spices, and in it put Antony's corpse. She then had a pit dug next to the shrine and had adders put in the pit. She had sworn to Antony, who had never been out of her thoughts day or night, to experience what he experienced, and to fulfill her vow, she leaped naked into the pit of adders.[12] Where Chaucer got the idea for this kind of death for her is unknown.[13]

Gower's account of Cleopatra in *Confessio Amantis* (1390-1393), "probably based on Chaucer,"[14] is but seven lines long; it also makes Cleopatra a martyr for love. The relevant lines are:

> Among these othre upon the grene
> I syh also the wofull queene
> Cleopatras, which in a Cave
> With Serpentz hath hirself begrave
> Alquik, and so sche was totore,
> For sorwe of that sche hadde lore
> Antonye, which hir love hath be.[15]

"Of all the stories that history has transmitted," Furness writes, "none possesses . . . such universal interest as a theme for dramatic tragedy as the loves of Antony and Cleopatra,"[16] and the seven plays on the subject in the sixteenth century[17] seem to bear out his claim. These dramatists, insofar as I can determine, continue the tradition of Cleopatra's loyalty to Antony.

Furness briefly describes some of the dramatic versions of the Cleopatra story written before May's play. Chronologically the first French tragedy and the first dramatic version of the story,[18] Estienne Jodelle's <u>Cleopatre Captive</u> (1552) shows her loyalty in her expression of loss at Antony's death:

> I've lost my lands, my kingdom,--and my all;
> And I have seen my life, and my support,
> My joy, my universe, take his own life![19]

For Furness, Jodelle's Cleopatra "is really touching in her simple misery, and in the plaintive confession of her many sins."[20]

In Robert Garnier's version of the story, <u>M. Antoine</u> (1578), translated by the Countess of Pembroke in 1592,

> Cleopatra appears in two Scenes, and what
> she is in the former she is in the latter,--
> a woman deeply in love with Antony, freely
> acknowledging that she entangled him in her
> snares ... and completely heart-broken that
> Antony should think she had been treacherous to him.[21]

Within two years Samuel Daniel, a member of the Countess of Pembroke's circle, wrote his closet and coterie drama <u>The Tragedie of Cleopatra</u> (1594).[22] It is not described by Furness but it shows a loyal Queen, one who even disclaims responsibility for pushing Antony into the war. Cleopatra says:

> Any my ambitious practises are thought
> The motive and the cause of all to be:
> Though God thou know'st, how just this
>   staine is layd

> Upon my soule, whom ill successe makes ill.[23]

In what Daniel's editor regards as an edition revised by Daniel and containing "unquestionably some of [his] finest work,"[24] the last two lines of the above quotation read:

> Though God thou knowst, this staine is wrongly laid
> Upon my soule....[25]

Cleopatra is so in love with Antony that, once he is dead, she says she has no reason to live except to "purchase grace / For my distressed seede after my death."[26] While Daniel's intention seems to be to show a loyal Queen, his play only takes up the story after Antony's death. In one passage Daniel suggests that Cleopatra might not have been entirely loyal, for he has her say about Antony:

> And even affliction makes me truely love thee.
> Which Antony, I must confesse my fault
> I never did sincerely untill now.[27]

This is the second suggestion in the literary tradition that Cleopatra's love might not be of a piece throughout. However, Furness believes that Daniel's play was of little influence; that Shakespeare was "in the faintest degree" influenced by it is "chimerical."[28]

Even if Shakespeare did not know Daniel's closet drama, the tradition of Cleopatra's loyalty to Antony and Antony's cause was well established by the time the dramatist turned to the story. Shakespeare did not depart from the tradition in his treatment of her character, because, according to Furness, she is constant in her loyalty to Antony. Furness correctly says that "the first words" spoken by Antony and Cleopatra "tell of boundless, illimitable love;" a love that "is maintained to the last throb of life in each of them." He further asserts that "never does Cleopatra waver in her wild and passionate love for Anthony."[29] Their love, however, excludes "passion and appetite;" indeed, "where in the play is there any proof of it?" and "where is there a word which, had it been addressed by a husband to a wife, we should not approve?"[30] Not only does Furness not see Cleopatra wavering in her conversations with Cæsar's messenger, but he even argues that she was trying to aid Antony's cause when she offered her services to Cæsar and held out treasure. He claims that when Cleopatra "kisses Cæsar's conquering hand, and kneels, with her crown, at his feet" she is following the "only course she could prudently take" to gain time for [Anthony] she must temporize with Cæsar."[31] Further, her holding out part of her treasure is not a sign that she intends to leave Antony, but it is "meant by her as a ruse to convince Cæsar that she had every intention of staying alive, and the fight with her treasurer [is] a put-up job."[32] The only "ocular proof" of her inconsistency occurs when Antony surprises Dolabella kissing her hand; Furness believes that her wistful reply to Antony's rage, "Not know me yet?" is but one more piece of evidence to justify his query, "Are we blind that we do not see that Shakespeare here means to show that Cleopatra has been throughout as true as steel to Anthony?"[33]

The literary tradition preceding May's version, then, portrays a loyal Cleopatra. The reasons for May's marked departure from the tradition are perhaps impossible to ascertain exactly, because no one can fully explain the process of artistic creation, but perhaps two broad reasons can be suggested. The treatment of the story in his acknowledged classical sources might have helped him interpret the events, and the intellectual climate in which he lived might have suggested that the story be interpreted in certain ways. Both reasons appear to be responsible for his new interpretation.

A brief examination of May's two important classical sources, which were carefully recorded as authorities in the margin of his manuscript and which interpret the story in two different ways, shows that he is highly dependent on them for his interpretation of Cleopatra's character. Of the six ancients claimed as authorities by May--Plutarch, Dio Cassius, Florus, Suetonius, Appian, and Strabo--Plutarch and Dio Cassius, who are credited far more often than any others, offer interpretations of the Antony and Cleopatra story which are different from each other. A description of first Plutarch's and then Dio Cassius's handling of certain details will show their different points of view.

For the dramatists of May's time, Furness claims that Plutarch was the common source.[34] Plutarch shows Cleopatra to be deeply in love with Antony and afraid of losing him. She wanted to accompany Antony to the wars because she feared that otherwise Octavia, Antony's wife and Octavius Cæsar's half-sister, would be able to reconcile Antony and Cæsar, and Antony would forsake his mistress.[35] Plutarch reports that the friendship of Thyreus, Cæsar's messenger, and Cleopatra made Antony jealous, so that Cleopatra, "to cleere her selfe of the suspicion he had of her, ...made more of him then ever she did."[36] Plutarch does not imply that Antony had any reason to be jealous. The historian also finds Cleopatra guiltless of surrendering Pelusium to Cæsar, claiming that the story that she did so was but a rumor. To clear herself of suspicion in this matter, Plutarch says, Cleopatra brought the wife and children of Seleucus, her officer in charge of the town, to Antony, "to be revenged of them at his pleasure."[37] Finally, Plutarch's description of Cleopatra's sorrow when Antony is dying shows the actions of a person overwrought by the death of a loved one. She

> layed [Antony] on a bed: she rent her
> garments upon him, clapping her brest,
> and scratching her face and stomake.
> Then she dried up his blood ... and
> called him her Lord, her husband, and
> Emperour, forgetting her owne miserie and calamity,
> for the pitie and compassion she tooke of
> him.[38]

She abused her body terribly while she buried Antony, raising "ulsers and inflamacions" on it;[39] she wept over his tomb, saying

> whilest we lived together, nothing could

> sever our companies: but now at our death,
> I feare me they will make us chaunge our
> countries.[40]

She prays the gods to "suffer not [Antony's] true frend and love to be carried away alive," asking to be buried with him in one tomb.[41] And the dying Antony had

> ernestly prayed [Cleopatra], and perswaded
> her, that she would seeke to save her life,
> if she could possible, without reproache and
> dishonor.[42]

While Plutarch shows an experienced, still-beautiful, and exciting woman enamored of and loyal to her lover, Dio Cassius, May's second important source, shows an experienced, still-beautiful schemer seeking every means to forward her own interests. After the battle at Actium had been lost, Cleopatra began plotting with Cæsar, because

> unknown to Antony, [she] sent to
> [Caesar] a golden scepter and a golden
> crown and the royal throne, through
> which she signified that she delivered
> the government to him. He might hate
> Antony, if he would only take pity on
> her. Cæsar accepted the gifts as a
> good omen, but made no answer to Antony.
> To Cleopatra he forwarded publicly threa-
> tening messages.... Secretly he sent
> word that, if she would kill Antony,

> he would grant her pardon and leave her
> empire unmolested.[43]

Clearly Dio Cassius intends to interpret character and events quite differently from Plutarch. Dio Cassius says, for example, that Cæsar took Pelusium by pretending to storm it, but the city had really been betrayed by Cleopatra,[44] and that when Cæsar marched on Alexandria, Cleopatra "secretly prevented the Alexandrians from making a sortie, though she pretended to urge them strongly to do so."[45] Whereas Plutarch says that Antony feared Cleopatra had betrayed him when he saw his troops yield to Cæsar, and Cleopatra fled to the tomb because she was afraid of Antony,[46] Dio Cassius says that Cleopatra ordered the ships to desert Antony and fled to the tomb, hoping that when he heard the false report of her death, he would not delay but take his own life.[47] She also selfishly tries to manipulate Cæsar after Antony's death, feigning one posture while really holding another.[48] Finally, Dio Cassius shows Cleopatra committing suicide in order to avoid the indignities of Cæsar's triumph,[49] while Plutarch shows Cleopatra praying the gods to

> suffer not [Antony's] true frend and
> lover to be caried away alive, that in
> me, they triumphe of [him.][50]

The only other ancient cited several times as an authority by May is Florus, whose brief account does not suggest that Cleopatra was disloyal to Antony. In his account, Cleopatra begs Cæsar for a portion of her kingdom only after Antony is dead.[51]

Thus the two acknowledged classical sources for May's play which treat the Cleopatra story at length offer different interpretations of her character. Plutarch shows a queen concerned about worldly affairs of course, but a captivating, intelligent, witty, charming, and beautiful consort for an aging yet great man. Dio Cassius shows a queen mainly concerned about advancing her own fortunes, unscrupulously using the love of an infatuated and easily led general to do it. Sometimes to the confusion of his play, especially in the character of Antony, May draws heavily on both sources.

Thus May's play is clearly dependent on Dio Cassius and Plutarch for its main outlines and partly dependent on Dio Cassius for its skeptical interpretation of Cleopatra's character. However, it also shows the skeptical spirit of May's age. His skepticism concerning the character of a person long famous in narrative and dramatic literature chiefly indicates his doubts about the abilities of men to remain steadfastly loyal when changes in fortune wrought by the accidents of history or men's actions and temperaments create situations in which loyalty and self-interest clash. May shows that but a minute fraction of men are capable of unselfish devotion, while most men choose the easier course. He does not condemn those who do waver or change their loyalty; the dilemma in which he places them and the choices he has them make demonstrate his underlying assumption that life requires men to commit themselves to absolute loyalties in a world made up of seemingly irreconcilable viewpoints. One is either for or against a man, a government, or a way of life, and that man, government, or way of life has somewhere its opposite, which also commands absolute loyalties. Some viewpoints are claimed to be more worthy than others, but the real reason for characters choosing one position over another is not the moral superiority of the new position, but rather the satisfaction of personal aims such as love, gain, or physical well-being.

While some characters utter traditional moral judgements of the conduct of others pursuing their selfish interest, the judgements do not convince the reader that May believed traditional moral patterns governed men's real conduct, partly because at times the characters making the evaluations are themselves suspect. When he required characters to choose between Antony or Cæsar, or between license or morality, he shows us characters adopting one loyalty or another without regard for traditional modes of judging men's actions. Those who change loyalties for selfish reasons are not condemned by those whom they forsake, those whom they join, or the higher powers, since retributive justice seems not to operate in the play. Those who remain loyal to Antony are but a handful; and although Antony praises their fidelity, the praise is hollow when loyalty brings them either death or a post in the enemies' camp no better or worse than the post they had before. To be faithfull is to die, as Eros and Cleopatra's servants show; to be disloyal is merely to change the color of one's coat.

The shifting loyalties of May's play even make Cleopatra's suicide not an act of fidelity--which is what she claims for it--but a selfish escape from her wretched future as a Roman captive. The dramatist makes clear by explicit statement that she chooses death as the alternative to captivity, and once death is all that is left for her, she as wholeheartedly devotes herself to Antony's memory as she, moments before, was devoted to furthering her earthly estate. Loyalty corresponds to self-interest for her at the end of the play, making her last act peculiarly ambiguous.

A detailed description of May's play will show that he places not only Cleopatra but also other characters in situations which require the choice of one loyalty or the other. Except for a handful, his characters are loyal for motives which either are unstated or ignoble. By making his characters choose between different loyalties, he reveals the demand of the late Jacobean age for decisions in real life requiring a choice between disparate loyalties, and by showing Cleopatra's selfish motives he shows his spirit is attuned to his age's skeptical view of the nature of women.

Cleopatra first appears to be an intelligent, charming and courtly mistress who commands and receives Antony's every attention, but who soon more truthfully shows herself as scheming and treacherous. Before her first appearance she is described by three of Antony's lieutenants as "a state beauty ... ordain'd by fate / to bee possest by them that rule the world."[52]

Further, "her Soule is full of greatnesse, and her witt / Has charms as many as her beauty has,"[53] but she is said to have "ambitious aimes,"[54] aims beyond Antony's gift of three kingdoms.[55] Antony, however, dotes on her: he compliments her beauty and her taste,[56] he foregoes examining letters from Rome in order not to "disturbe the pleasures of [the] night,"[57] he debases a king to honor her,[58] and he makes a gift to her of a famous library.[59]

In return for his trust she selfishly hires Antony's lieutenant Canidius to persuade Antony that she ought to accompany him to the war because she fears that she will lose her "state ... hopes and fortunes" if Octavia should successfully intercede between husband and brother a second time.[60] Cleopatra hides her real reason for going by pleading that her love for Antony urges her to be "a partner in his highest cares," a partner "whose soule hee [thinks] ... fitt to share / In all his dangers."[61] Antony believes her. When she gets her way, she says aside, "My wishes are effected,"[62] sounding like the scheming villain of a melodrama. She repays Antony's confidence in her courageous heart by fleeing from the battle,[63] feigning victory when she lands in Egypt,[64] offering "herselfe, and all her fortunes to [Cæsar's] service"[65] soon after landing in Egypt, and offering to Cæsar, in return for her liberty and the crown of Egypt for herself and her children, a "great masse of gold" which she has hidden "unknowne t' Antonius."[66]

Thus she is correctly described by Agrippa as a Queen with

an "ambition greater than her fortunes"[67] who has ruled "halfe
the Roman world, / Trodd on the necks of humbled kings,"[68]
and is possessed of a "haughty spirit" that "will never stoope
[to] captivity."[69] Her "haughty spirit" leads her to seek a
poison that first will enable her to "controll the spite
of Fortune"[70] and second to save herself from servitude[71] and
loss of honor;[72] but only as a last resort will she die,
because her aim is to achieve such eminence that "her glorious
name" will be "fix[ed]... above the starrs."[73] No longer
does Antony serve her purpose; the agent who will now achieve
this greatness for her is Cæsar, and controll of Cæsar is
to be gained by her beauty. In short, she will sell herself to
the highest bidder.

Her double dealing reaches a climax in Act IV. After seeking
to "devise seom meanes ... to deserve great Cæsar's love,"[74]
she, seconds later, addresses Antony, just returned from Pharos,
as "my dearest lord;"[75] assuring him that his welcome feast,
"the feast of fellow-dyers," shows the "firme" bond of those who
"live in love, that meane to dy togither."[76] Antony's acceptance
of her statement exemplifies Miss Ellis-Fermor's claim that "the
sense of defeat ... was so marked a characteristic of the
Jacobeans."[77] Believing her, Antony has no reason to suspect
that she commands Pelusium to be "rendred upp to Cæsar"[78] except
that his lieutenants expose the treachery of Cæsar's messenger
Thyreus. But when Antony accuses her of treachery, she claims
"a faithfull heart,"[79] threatening to use the asp, which she is
keeping as a "preservative / 'Gainst Cæsar's cruelty,""against

Antonius' baseness, a worse foe / Then Cæsar is."[80] Antony callowly relents, fawning on her before leaving for a final attack on Cæsar.

When the false report of her death causes Antony to slay himself, she does not mourn Antony, but is torn by doubts about her future. She says that "knowne mischiefes have their cure; but doubts none;" she prefers "despair" to "fruitless hope Mixt with a killing feare."[81] She would willingly choose either an honorable life or death, but she cannot live in an undetermined position. Her "doubting soule" is "afflict[ed]" to know whether Caesar's "love will proove/ Feigned or true."[82] The reader knows which alternative was long before decided on; the dramatist constructs a situation which holds the reader's attention not by doubt about the outcome, but because men's actions, temperaments, and the accidents of history demand that a character choose between alternate absolute positions--between life or death. Once she sees that the situation will not allow her to pursue her selfish interests, and that she has no honorable way out, she chooses immediately.

The situation is striking in Act V because Cleopatra clearly prefers death to doubt, a known position to a non-determined position. Her long temptation scene with Cæsar shows her begging for death rather than the indeterminate, doubtful future of a captive in Rome, and after she sees no sign of love in Cæsar, she cryptically replies to the question "How fares youre Majesty?" by saying "never so well-- / As now I am."[83] That is, she now knows that she will not be empress of the world

but must choose either captivity or death. With two choices
open to her, she has no fears about preferring death to a life
of dishonor. Once she is resolved, she wholeheartedly commits
herself to her new role which in fact results from a selfish
choice but which appears to be loyalty to Antony; she now claims
to be Antony's loving and loyal mistress. She truthfully
says that she was "never till now [his] true and faithfull
love;"[84] and once she decides, all other alternatives are
forgotten. With the greatest pomp she dies so that she can "begge
[his] pardon in the other world."[85]

Cleopatra's motives are not difficult to determine; throughout the play she has but one end in view: to be empress of the world, to be "the Queene of fortune."[86] She cannot know which general to cast her lot with until the final battle shows the victor, because presumably Cæsar, who appears ascendant, could by chance die in the final skirmishes. Thus she barters with Cæsar while feigning loyalty to Antony. Cleopatra articulates her dilemma; should Antony win, he would find out she has been treacherous; should Cæsar win, she is unsure of his love because she has only dealt with his messenger. Her solution is "to make all sure"[87] by going to the tomb; when she does so she is <u>not</u> the queen of fortune because she says:

> If fates contrive
> A future state of happinesse for mee,
> It is my castle; if my death they doome,
> I am possest already of a tombe.[88]

The alternatives are clear: either happiness or death.

Clearly, Cleopatra is not loyal to Antony. The dramatist places her in situations which show her scheming to gain her own selfish goals; he shows her claiming loyalty to Antony while bartering with Cæsar. If she loves Antony she ought to be against Cæsar, but she is not; if she is against Antony, she ought to be for Cæsar, but she is not. In her attempt to bestride the twin colossi of Antony and Cæsar lies the focal point of the play. She wants to be the manipulator of both men, the queen of fortune who operates through the agencies of Rome's ostensible rulers. She can be said to be continually loyal only to herself; she uses the doting Antony for her own gain, and she would use Cæsar, if she could but ensnare him, for the same end. Her "ambitious aimes" seek to control the world through the figurehead who has her momentary loyalty. Three great Romans have so far been her lovers; she had just as soon add a fourth.

Thus after Actium the reader's interest is fixed not on the fortunes of Antony--he is obviously finished--but on the writhings of Cleopatra to free herself from the grasp of fortune. She attempts to control her destiny, but in fact she does little to alter the irrevocable course of events after Actium. She has no chance against Cæsar from the beginning: he sees through her letter at once, concerned only not to lose the gold she offers while also keeping her alive to adorn his triumph.[89] Cleopatra, however, half believes the courtings of Cæsar's glib messenger Thyreus, who calls her "the Queen of fortune" who holds "a lasting scepter ore that fickle Goddesse."[90]

Other characters also vacillate in their loyalty to Antony. Early in the play Titius and Plancus flee to Cæsar with their forces, and are soon joined by Domitius, Silanus, Dellius, and Hipparchus, "fortunes frends," not Antony's.[91] Further, after the loss at Actium, Pinnarius Scarpus persuades his soldiers to join Cæsar.[92] Antony is finally left with but three faithful friends, Eros, Lucilius, and Aristocrates.

Not only is the treachery of Antony's lieutenants reprehensive if judged by traditional morality, but the motives for it also are traditionally reprehensible. In the first act Plancus and Titius, two of Antony's lieutenants who fell to Cæsar, object to Antony's Alexandrian triumph "to honor Cleopatra's pride,"[93] to his forsaking Octavia, "his lawfull wife,"[94] to not daring to counsel Antony,[95] to his revelling which they fear makes him soft,[96] to his amorous language,[97] to his inattention about state letters,[98] to his giving away three kingdoms,[99] to his debasing Atavasdes,[100] to his bestowing the library of Pergamus on Cleopatra,[101] and to his will, which would have his body interred in Alexandria.[102] Their list of Antony's lapses is impressive, yet when Plancus and Titius explain why they treacherously take their forces and leave Antony, they do not adduce these lapses but say they fear he might not resign his absolute power after Cæsar's defeat, they will not fight to make Cleopatra "mistress of the world and him," and they have endured "scornes and wrongs" at Cleopatra's hands.[103] Of their three reasons, two are but doubts about the future, and the third is never shown. Why do they really leave Antony? Because Rome "favours Cæsar much;"[104] because, that is, Caesar's star apparently is ascendant and Antony's is descendant, and they want to be on the winning side. Other characters say nothing about their treason, and even Antony makes no comment at all when he hears that they have fled; Canidius but observes, "you shall not neede theire help...at all."[105]

After the loss at Actium, as is to be expected, other lieutenants flee to Cæsar. Pinnarius Scarpus pursuades his soldiers to join Cæsar by arguing that they are "discharg'd from all obedience" owed Antony "by fate it selfe"[105] because the "Godds themselves ordaine[d]" Cæsar's victory.[107] His specious argument intends to get him on the side of the winner; smart money does not bet on a loser.

Thus Antony's lieutenants forsake him with the hope of improving their lot in life, as presumably they do, but those who remain loyal, Lucilius and Aristocrates, receive exactly the same reward: acceptance into Cæsar's service. Retributive justice does not seem to operate, and no one condemns the self-seekers for their actions.

Once Cleopatra makes certain basic decisions—to go to the wars with Antony or not; to flee the battle or not; to abandon Antony for Cæsar or not—she seems unable to alter the events the decisions set in motion. Perhaps because once choices are made the resulting events seem to be inevitable, the characters are not brought to judgment for choosing one loyalty or another, or for the motives that occasioned their choices. While the possibility of choice is present, chance and fate seem to be

equally responsible for determining events. May does not take
a clear stand on the question of whether one freely chooses and
so determines events, or whether events determine a person's
choice.

His characters invariably attribute the cause of things to
Fate or Fortune, as in Cleopatra's farewell to life:

> Alas, I did not sway
> A scepter over Fortune, or command
> As now I doo, the Destinyes themselves.[108]

Because she holds certain death in her hands, she believes that
finally she controls fate, instead of being controlled by it. But
she is deceived, for the events of the play have shown that her
every effort has been to avert the end that fate reserved for her.
May clearly shows--with good precedent in Dio Cassius and
Plutarch of course--that fortune operated in the lives of men.
He uses 116 lines in Act II, Scene iv to describe the portents
observed by Egyptians and Romans before Actium, ending the
scene with the ritual prognostication by Achoreus, Cleopatra's
priest, of the certainty of a change of government in Egypt.
Nearly all the portents are found in one or another of May's
classical sources; that he included so many at such length, and
that he elsewhere in the play frequently mentions the importance
of the governing power of fate over the lives and actions of
men shows his general use of the notion. As Canidius says
in the first scene,

> It was the crime of us and fate it selfe

> That <u>Antony</u> and Cæsar would usurpe
> A power so great.[109]

The wheel of Fortune in May's play shows Cæsar ascending and Antony and Cleopatra descending; the aspiring Cæsar has seized on Fortune's forelock, while Antony and Cleopatra are subject to unfavorable unregulated accidents. Thus Cleopatra calls her love for Antony "fates owne crime;" she tells Cæsar that had fate allotted Egypt to his protection, she would have been his "frend" instead,[110] and she would have poisons so that she can control Fortune herself.[111] The priest Achoreus, after prophesying the ruin of Egypt, urges the wise man to find strength

> within himself...
> That whatsoever from the Godds can come
> May finde him ready to receive theire doome.[112]

Nothing can be done to avert it. Thus a rigidity of cause and effect governs the actions of men, and if one seeks the original cause of a series of events, he is driven ever backwards.

The Tudor historians show a similar rigidity of cause and effect in the Wars of the Roses, and Shakespeare's plays on the subject reflect their view. Given a certain kind of character or situation, the outcome must be of a certain kind. So in <u>Richard II</u> lies the difficulty of determining Richard's original error: what was the action that, once made, set off the irrevocable series of events? The view of men as the star's tennis balls, in Bosola's phrase, is not an uncommon one in the age of Elizabeth. As the Duchess of Malfi says,

> When Fortune's wheel is overcharg'd with Princes,

The waight makes it move swift.[113]

The soothsayer in Act I, Scene ii of Shakespeare's <u>Antony and Cleopatra</u> likewise suggests that everything is already decided for the important characters. Danby remarks that in <u>Philaster</u> Arethusa's "inversion of propriety is justified by invoking the overruling power of the gods: "'tis the gods / The gods that make me so';"[114] Salingar claims that the theme of incest in '<u>Tis Pity</u> "is not analysed psychologically but is presented as a supreme case of star-cross'd lovers, essentially the same in kind as that of Romeo and Juliet;"[115] Sensebaugh demonstrates that scientific necessity controls the actions of Ford's characters and says "but whatsoever man's state, all is determined; whatever he is or hopes to become is the result of a formula not of his making;"[116] May, in his tragedy <u>Agrippina</u>, has Narcissus say

> Since wee must fall, it is some happinesse
> To fall the honest way, if wee may call
> That honesty at all, or reall vertue
> To which necessity enforces us,
> And wee by fortune not election practise;[117]

and Plutarch, finally, after showing how Cleopatra persuaded Antony to let her go to the war, says,

> These fayer perswasions wan him: for it
> was predestined that the government of all the
> world should fall into Octavius Cæsars handes.[118]

Miss Ellis-Fermor correctly claims that the Jacobean dramatists show "man doomed to destruction by the gods."[119]

Likewise, May shows that the general scheme of action in the play is governed by a fate that men cannot control. Yet individual men can and do at times elect to change their course of action when it is to their advantage in this world to do so. But only the minor figures are allowed this privilege; for Antony, Cleopatra, and Cæsar, every effort to arrange their life proves futile. Cæsar, for example, orders an attack on Pelusium, but we later hear that the town was surrendered on Cleopatra's command to gain his favor. His complex efforts to prevent Cleopatra's death come to naught. Antony for no good reason flees the sea battle, which he might have won, to follow Cleopatra, and fails to press his advantage on land when, even after losing at sea, he might have won there. Cleopatra unmercifully plays Antony off to gain Cæsar's favor but fails to get it when analogy and experience ought to prove her successful. Minor characters, however, switch their loyalty from Antony to Cæsar and suffer nothing for it.

May pays lip service to the traditional virtues, but, as I have shown, the characters who remain loyal get nothing for their efforts. Plutarch, however, shows that treason is punished when he describes what happened to Alexas, who was sent by Antony to Herod to keep Herod Loyal, but treacherously persuaded Herod to support Cæsar:

> Howbeit Herodes did him no pleasure: for
> he was presently taken prisoner, and sent in chaines

> his owne countrie, and there by Cæsar
> commaundement put to death. Thus was
> Alexas in Antonius life time put to
> death, for betraying him.[120]

And in Daniel's *Cleopatra*, Seleucus to his dismay finds he is hated by the person to whom he gives secrets:

> My treachery is quitted with disgrace,
> My falshood loath'd...yet Princes in this case
> Doe hate the Traitor, though they love the treason.[121]

A statement made by Knights about *Sejanus* accurately describes May's *Cleopatra*, especially the condemnation of Antony by his lieutenants in Act I. Knights says that "the 'good' characters are choric and denunciatory merely, representing no positive values."[122] Early in May's play, for example, Canidius says about criticism of Antony,

> Tis envy not morality that makes
> You taxe his love, how gravely ere you talk.[123]

Later, when Cæsar says "wee ever lov'd fidelity"[124] while accepting into his service Antony's two loyal captains Aristocrates and Lucilius after Antony's death, we suspect that he loves fidelity to himself only, not Fidelity as a virtue; his lavish praise of the dead Antony has been discredited by the judgement of the two faithful captains when Lucilius says aside about Cæsar's show of grief, "Most royall *Cæsar*-like dissimulation."[125] But the loyalty of the captains must not be discredited; Antony's farewell to the faithful assures us that their "faith and manly constancy upbraides / This wicked age, and shall enstruct the next."[126]

As Thomas May's literary production indicates, and as is to be expected of a writer clearly not of the first rank, he followed the lead of his more gifted contemporaries, trying his hand at tragedies on classical themes as Shakespeare and Jonson had tried theirs; he wrote smart comedies of London life; he translated Latin masters into English; and he wrote histories for pay.[127] His play about Cleopatra clearly shows his dependence on Shakespeare's Antony and Cleopatra for its construction (the events of both plays are similar, and Act I, for example, follows the same pattern in both plays) and more importantly his dependence on Beaumont and Fletcher for his underlying assumptions.

The publication in 1623 of the first folio of Shakespeare's plays and the subsequent editions of the folio attest that Shakespeare's genius was recognized by his immediate successors. If his plays were highly regarded, however, they were not as often performed as the plays of Beaumont and Fletcher were after Shakespeare's death. Stage records show that from 1616 to 1642 the King's Men played at court 113 times. Of these performances, 43 were of Beaumont and Fletcher plays, while but 16 were of Shakespeare and only 7 of Jonson. Further, of the 170 plays known to be on their active list during these years, 47 were Beaumont and Fletcher plays, 16 Shakespeare's, and 9 Jonson's.[128] May, who attached himself to the court of James, probably shared the taste of his contemporaries for Beaumont and Fletcher.

That many Beaumont and Fletcher plays were successful box office attractions is not hard to understand because they exhibit characteristics which make for popular success: striking situations, surprising plots, variety of easily understood characters, and superior verse. But that Beaumont and Fletcher were regarded by many of their contemporaries as superior to Shakespeare does require explanation. In some way, that is, the Jacobeans felt that Beaumont and Fletcher were closer to them, spoke more directly to them. Perhaps the explanation is to be found not only in the jaded tastes of a less broadly popular, more aristocratic audience, but also is to be found in the appeal their underlying viewpoint had. As J. F. Danby points out,

> in history as in the Beaumont drama the
> setting for the main actors was one in
> which all-or-nothing and either-or were
> continually presented as the alternatives
> for choice. The absolutes of Justice for the subject,
> Loyalty to the King, Faith in God,
> Obedience to Church Discipline--a medly
> of incompatible demands surrounded the
> individual.[129]

Trevelyan supports Danby's observation when he says about James' view of the Kingship that the attempt "to materialize English King-worship into the political dogma of divine and

> hereditary right...split its essence in the dust;" the Stuarts adopted policies at home and abroad which were...opposed to the wishes of the strongest elements in English society. The situation thus created forced to the front claims on behalf of the house of Commons which were as new to the constitution as the claims of divine hereditary right and autocratic power on behalf of the Crown.[130]

James further forced his subjects into the position of either being for or against him when he "dismiss[ed] all judges who dared to interpret the laws impartially."[131] And in religious matters, when, Trevelyan feels, a compromise might easily have been reached by "widening...the borders of a State Church designed to be elastic," James declared "No Bishop, no King," and added "'I shall make them conform themselves or I will harry them out of the land.'"[132] One either had to be for or against the policies of James. Thus Trevelyan's comments about the politics and religious views of James appear to bear out Danby's claim that the reign of James was

> a time when action was demanded on the basis of the conviction entertained; when loyalties were being solicited by widely different authorities.[133]

Dramatists writing for a courtly audience might well reflect in their plays the demands real life was making on men, and a

courtier dramatist such as May, following the lead of his popular
contemporaries, could hardly fail to register in his plays the
views of his time. Conversely, the popular dramatists might
well help shape the view of their audience; "later people,"
that is

> play out Beaumont-and-Fletcherism in their
> own biographies. Kenelm Digby is one of
> their heroes in the flesh. The early part
> of Herbert of Cherbury's autobiography
> reads like one of their plays.[134]

In their plays Beaumont and Fletcher created situations in
which absolute views conflict and characters choose one
loyalty or the other, without moral conflict. Philaster, for
example, recognizes on the one hand the King and on the other
the demand for justice by the spirit of his father, but he is not
engaged in a moral conflict because of the demands:

> he can live...in either the one loyalty
> or the other because committal removes
> the need for moral deliberation and
> supervenes on conflict by suppression
> of one of the warring terms.[135]

Typical Beaumont and Fletcher situations "turn on divisions
that such rival absolutes bring about when the central characters find themselves between...them,"[136] and the situations
"leave behind them various and quite discrete bases on which the
separate stances, monumental or heroic, can be taken."[137]

Further, the Beaumont hero is "fated,"
> he is cut off from the social past and
> the neighbourly present and his future
> includes only death. He is absolved from
> the need to exert rational control, and
> incapable of compromise. He is self-
> enclosed in the splintering world of
> contending absolutes, and all the
> violence and activity these call out
> can only end in self-destruction. The
> fated lover-hero of the Beaumont drama is
> one of the great premonitory symbols of
> the seventeenth century.[138]

The description not only suits the Beaumont hero, but also precisely describes Antony in nearly every detail.

Danby's explication of both <u>Philaster</u> and <u>The Maid's Tragedy</u> is remarkably successful and strikes a note that rings true. Whether May had the perspicuity to recognize the Beaumont hero or the Beaumont and Fletcher viewpoint and followed these dramatists alone, or whether his sources lie elsewhere, one cannot of course determine. But as his biographer Chester continually asserts, and as his literary work testifies, he willingly drifted with the currents of his time.

I have shown that some of the characters in <u>Cleopatra</u> adopt one role or another with equal ease, choosing first this stance and then another. The diction of the first eight lines

of the play points to a conflict of absolutes; words of opposite
meanings are paired: "shame and dishonour / triumph";[139]
honour /pride"'[140] "ruine / pleasure";[141] "jest / prophecy";[142]
"sadd / merry."[143] But May's interest lies in situations, not
in depth of character, and in those situations which show characters
choosing one course of action or the other. Circumstances,
not character, hold our interest. May cites Florus as one of
his historical sources, and in Florus the extreme stances
adopted by Antony are made clear:

> After the Parthian expedition he acquired
> a loathing for war and lived a life of ease,
> and a slave to his love for Cleopatra,
> rested in her royal arms as though all had
> gone well with him. The Egyptian woman demanded
> the Roman Empire from the drunken general as the price
> of her favours; and this Antonius promised her.[144]

Florus shows Antony moving from the role of the unsuccessful yet
beloved general to the slave of love; from the general concerned
about each of his soldiers to the drunken sot giving away an
empire for a harlot's bed. The extremity of stances forced on
Antony and the machinations of Cleopatra made their story
suitable for a Jacobean dramatist trying to cater to his age.

Thus in the sudden and unmotivated change of loyalty,
passion, or mood in his characters, and in the use of Fate as
a partial explanation for the working out of events, May's
play shows itself dependent on his contemporaries. But the play

also reflects a new skepticism about the nature of women; a skepticism seen elsewhere, for example, in hortatory epistles to sons, and in the actions and beliefs of members of the court.

The precepts to their sons by Lord Burghley (1561 and ca. 1584),[145] Sir Walter Raleigh (ca. 1603),[146] and Francis Osborne (ca. 1648)[147] were well-known and popular.[148] Their advice shows an increasing cynicism in regard to women on the part of the three writers. Raleigh is more cynical than Burghley, and Osborne is more cynical than Raleigh. Indeed, as Louis B. Wright says in his introduction to a recent collection of the precepts, booksellers in Oxford were forbidden by the Vice-Chancellor of the University from selling Osborne's book because of its cynical comments.[149] The precepts are useful as evidence because they show that, as the seventeenth century progressed, a skeptical view about the nature of women became clear.

Burghley, for example, briefly advises his son Robert to choose a wife carefully, "for from thence may spring all thy future good or ill."[150] Inquiry should be made of her disposition and of her parents; she should not be poor nor ill-favored.[151] She should, in short, be carefully chosen, but Burghley refrains from explicit comment about the ills that befall from a poor choice. Most important, he does not denigrate marriage, but assumes that naturally and desirably a young man should marry.

Raleigh, however, says that while affections do not last, the marriage contract does; therefore affections are

> better to be borne withal in a mistress
> than in a wife, for when thy humor shall
> change thou art yet free to choose again.[152]

Beauty fades; it "will neither last nor please thee one year" because desire dies when the object is attained. Notwithstanding, the wife should be fair so the offspring will not be ugly. He believes that all poor but fair women are made dishonest sooner or later, and that all young wives betray old husbands. Despite his reservations, Raleigh believes that women can and do truly love men, and that ideally the man should be beloved of the wife rather than be "besotted on her;" the tests of her love are her care of her husband's estate and her desire to please without instruction.[153]

Osborne, born in 1593, two years before Thomas May, went as a young country gentleman to London, where he was a member of the court circle, holding minor posts.[154] Like the rest of his treatise, his views about women, written in 1648, conceivably reflect fairly accurately the "motivations and the ideas of Osborne's segment of society."[155] And his views are cynical:

> Eve, by stumbling at the serpent's
> solicitations, cast her husband out of
> paradise. Nor are her daughters surer of
> foot, being foundered by the heat of
> lust and pride and unable to bear the
> weight of so much of our reputation as
> religion and custom hath loaded them
> withal, that an unballasted behavior

without other leakage is sufficient to
cast away an husband's esteem.[156]

The implied comparison of the nature of women to a mare in heat, carried out even to the physical manifestation of the mare's condition, is unsavory enough; but when he abuses beauty and argues for marrying rich, he says

> I have heard a well-built woman compared
> in her motion to a ship under sail. Yet
> I would advise no wise man to be her owner
> if her fraight be nothing but what she
> carries between wind and water.[157]

Children are no reason for marriage, as Burghley and Raleigh believed, but rather the "careful looks of all fathers give evidence to the truth of that saying, 'Children are uncertain comforts but certain troubles'."[158] His final advice, Wright says, "reduces to a whine the Queen of Carthage's tragic lamentations over Aeneas' desertion:"[159]

> Therefore, dear son, if you find yourself
> smitten with this poisoned dart, imitate
> his prudence who chose rather to cast himself
> into the arms of the sea and travel
> than to let his hopes and parts wither
> in those of a poor whining Dido,
> who is no more able to give you caution
> for the continuance of her own affection
> than you are of yours or of her beauty.[160]

Since the accepted date for May's play is 1626,[161] the

best evidence for demonstrating that a new skepticism about
women resulted in part from the actions and beliefs of ladies of
the court ideally ought to precede May's play in date. However,
surely ideals of character and conduct are not formed overnight;
if Henrietta Maria found English courtiers and ladies amenable
to her ideals of courtly love, as she did, the ground must have
been prepared for the seed. As Wright says about the letters
of advice to sons,

> The ideals of character and conduct
> represented by the earlier courtesy
> books of the Renaissance like Castig-
> lione's Book of the Courtier had now
> given way to pragmatic handbooks of
> success.[162]

I am not suggesting that the reign of James I was characterized
by moral laxity, but that certain beliefs and historical events
foreshadowed the real excesses of the court of Charles I.

Petrarchanism, for example, remained for a great number
of years as a viable literary convention; the question to ask
about it is why it was able to remain useful for such a long
time. Literary fads die relatively quickly; but Petrarchanism
offered a means of circumventing the reason-passion, body-soul
conflict typical of the Renaissance by enabling the speaker
and the recipient of the poem to pretend that satisfaction was
never to be achieved, while the neo-Platonic code of courtly
love, intimately tied up with Petrarchanism, enabled the lover
to pretend that his lust was in fact something else. Sonnet

sequences dependent on the Petrarchan convention remained popular in the first quarter of the seventeenth century; Drayton, for example, revised Idea's Mirror continually for eleven editions from 1594 to his death in 1631,[163] and neo-Platonic notions are commonplace in the poetry of Spenser and Donne.

Historical evidence for corruption in the court of James is not abundant. Perhaps the most infamous event is the visit to London in 1606 of the Danish King Christian IV, described by John Harington. In a letter to Barlow, Harington described some of the "carousal and sports" he observed, claiming that

> the great ladies do go well-masked, and indeed it be the only show of their modesty to conceal their countenance.[164]

The ladies "abandon[ed] their sobriety," Harington said, and were "seen to roll about in intoxication."[165] If his condemnation is made so generally as to be suspect, his details amply support his assertion. He reports on a "representation" of Solomon and the Queen of Sheba made by court ladies, describing how the Danish King wanted to dance with the Queen of Sheba, who had just stumbled drunkenly, dumping "wine, cream, jelly, [and] beverage" on his lap, but the King "fell down...and was carried to an inner chamber, and laid on a bed of state." Later, Hope, Faith, and Charity entered "in rich dress" but Hope and Faith were too drunk to speak their lines; Charity spoke only briefly before joining the other two who "were both sick and spewing in the lower hall."[166]

In 1611 Lord Thomas Howard, in a letter to Harington, describes the vanity of James and the foppery of the court so Harington will know how to act when he comes to London. Most telling is Howard's description of the favorite Robert Carr, and the comment:

> I know those would not quietly reste,
> were Carr to leer on their wives, as
> some do perceive, yea, and like it well
> too they should be so noticed.[167]

Lord Herbert of Cherbury makes the commonplace satiric remark that in 1608 he "resorted to court" without being "tainted with those corrupt delights incident to the times,"[168] but satirists attacked the court more viciously. Whether the charges of the satirists were literally true or whether because of the genre of "biting" satire the charges were exaggerated is an open question. Sensebaugh, however, believes that the satirists aimed at real laxity, because he piles up an impressive amount of evidence from the satirists to show that the court was in fact a place of sexual looseness.[169]

The accession to the throne of Charles I in 1626, and his marriage to Henrietta Maria the same year, supposedly signalled the arrival in England of the "new" code of courtly love. Sensebaugh claims that the Queen brought a new mode of behavior with her,[170] but as Danby points out, "the inner core" of Beaumont and Fletcher plays,

> wherein the novelty consists, and in
> which the main seriousness of the drama-

> tists is displayed, is the platonic or
> petrarchan triangle of the lovers.[171]

Salingar also argues for the presence in English plays of courtly ideals before 1626, when he says that whether the tragic heroes of post-Elizabethan plays

> storm or languish, like Philaster, or
> 'hold it as commendable to be wealthy in
> pleasure / As others do in rotten sheep and
> pasture,' like the rake in Fletcher's
> comedy, they are all of them Cavalier
> gallants idealized, and their adventures
> move invariably on the plane of love and
> honour.[172]

Danby explicitly argues for the Petrarchan convention in Beaumont's lovers, who love without return, without "a mutual contract," in "a private direction of the will," so that the lover is "completely insulated within his love."[173]

Therefore I argue that the English court and the English dramatists were well prepared for Henrietta Maria, when in 1628 the cult of Platonic love in her court "was just beginning to take shape,"[174] and that events shortly after the performance of May's play count as evidence for a new skepticism about the nature of women.

> The ideals of beauty and love held by the new Queen were
> reminiscent of the sonnets of Petrarch,
> of sixteenth century Italian pastorals,
> of Spanish romances, [and] of French

Renaissance poetry and prose.[175]
These ideals, Sensebaugh claims, were soon

> buzzed about and debated as matters of
> utmost importance, and shortly various
> forms of literature began to reflect
> the discussion.[176]

Sensebaugh cogently argues for a considerable influence on literature as well as life by the ideas of the cult. He claims that "groups modeled after the Queen's coterie sprang up in courts of minor importance," and that "many court plays were written for the specific purpose of making clear the philosophy of the cult." These "manifestations" describe "in some measure its manners and morals" and thus enable Sensebaugh to "compile the code of love."[177]

The code is in its eight points partially descriptive of the events of May's play. The eight points listed by Sensebaugh are:

1. Fate rules all lovers.
2. Beauty and goodness are one and the same.
3. Beautiful women are saints to be worshipped.
4. True love is of equal hearts and divine.
5. Love is all-important and all-powerful.
6. True love is more important than marriage.
7. True love is the sole guide of virtue.
8. True love allows any liberty of action and thought.[178]

The first point is abundantly clear in May's play; the second and third not so clear. Yet Cleopatra is a "good" for Antony, to be held at any cost, and his adoration of her, a blind dotage, amounts to worship. His recognition of and her claims for equality, point four, occur when he consents to her arguments for accompanying him to Actium; further, the reports of their gambols in Alexandria show their equality if not divinity. Dryden recognized the existence of the fifth point in their story when he titled his play <u>All for Love, or, The World Well Lost</u>. Antony's abandoning of Octavia, who so loyally supported him in Rome during the years of his absence, amply illustrates the sixth point, that true love is more important than marriage, as it does in a sense the eighth, that true love allows any liberty of action and thought, but the seventh point, that true love is the sole guide to virtue, only implicitly exists in the play. For Antony's very reason for being in Alexandria, for warring on Cæsar, for abandoning wife and family is "true love"; because of his love he only can pursue certain courses of action which, if his love tells him are desirable, must, within the terms of his love, be "virtuous." Thus the absence of a viable traditional morality by which to judge the actions of Antony and Cleopatra can perhaps be accounted for.

Samuel Daniel ended his <u>Cleopatra</u> with the Chorus asking two complementary yet contradictory questions:

> Is greatnesse of this sort,
> That greatnesse greatnesse marres,
> And wrackes it selfe, selfe-driven

>   On Rockes of her owne might?
>
>   Doth Order order so
>
>   Disorders overthrow?[179]

The questions get at one of the reasons that make the story of Antony and Cleopatra infinitely greater than a report of a sordid extra-marital affair. The chief personages are "great" in several ways: in their positions in the world, in the power of their passion to make their actions right through wrong, and in the sheer extravagance of their risk--they lose nothing less than the world. "Greatnesse" of "this sort," one believes, has power enough to drive itself on the rocks if it should desire to do so; but the question asked by the Chorus implies that greatness paradoxically mars itself, seeks to destroy its own self. The expense by which greatness is achieved is thus a waste; man's efforts come to naught if greatness in overweening pride destroys itself. But the second question suggests that the reach of greatness is shortened by the yet more powerful unifying principle of Order, which "overthrow[s]" the Disorder wrought by greatness. Thomas May shows us that while greatness both wastefully mars itself and is subject to the principle of Order, the pattern of history exemplified in the story of Antony and Cleopatra satisfies our desire for completeness-- for a resolution demonstrating that principle which underlies man's attempt to organize his world through the medium of art.

Footnotes

¹H. H. Furness, ed., *The Tragedie of Anthonie and Cleopatra*, in a *New Variorum Edition of Shakespeare*, 22 vols. (Philadelphia, 1907), XV, 521.

²Una Ellis-Fermor, *Jacobean Drama*, 4th ed. (London, 1961), p. 10.

³H. S. Bennett, *Chaucer and the Fifteenth Century* (New York, 1947), p. 140.

⁴*Lydgate's Fall of Princes*, ed. Henry Bergen, 4 vols. (Washington, D.C., 1923), III, 772-773, ll. 3620-3628.

⁵Giovanni Boccaccio, *Concerning Famous Women*, trans. Guido A. Guarino (New Brunswick, N.J., 1963), p. 195.

⁶*Ibid*., p. 193.

⁷*Ibid*., p. 194.

⁸*Ibid*.

⁹*Ibid*.

¹⁰*Ibid*., p. 195.

¹¹F. N. Robinson, ed., *The Works of Geoffrey Chaucer*, 2d ed. (Boston, 1957), p. 482.

¹²*Ibid*., pp. 496-497.

¹³Ibid., p. 848, n. for ll. 678-680, 696-702.

¹⁴*Ibid*., p. 846.

¹⁵*The English Works of John Gower*, ed. G.C. Macaulay, 2 vols.,in *Early English Text Society*, Extra Series, No. 81-82 (London, 1901), 82, p. 456, Bk. 8, ll. 2571-2577.

¹⁶Furness, p. xvii.

¹⁷M.W. MacCallum, *Shakespeare's Roman Plays* (London, 1910), p. 310.

¹⁸Furness, p. xvii.

¹⁹*Ibid*., p. 507.

[20] Ibid., p. xix.

[21] Ibid., p. 511.

[22] In *The Complete Works in Verse and Prose of Samuel Daniel*, Ed. Alexander B. Grosart, 5 vols. (London, 1885-1896), III.

[23] Ibid., pp. 36-37, ll. 117-120.

[24] Ibid., p. 19.

[25] Ibid., p. 37.

[26] Ibid., p. 35, ll. 150-152.

[27] Ibid., p. 38, ll. 150-152.

[28] Furness, p. 515.

[29] Ibid., p. xi.

[30] Ibid., p. xiv.

[31] Ibid., p. xii.

[32] Ibid., p. xiii.

[33] Ibid., p. xii.

[34] Ibid., p. xviii.

[35] *Plutarch's Lives of the Noble Grecians and Romans*, trans. Sir Thomas North, 6 vols. (London, 1896), VI, 58.

[36] Ibid., p. 76.

[37] Ibid., p. 77.

[38] Ibid., p. 80.

[39] Ibid., p. 84.

[40] Ibid., p. 86.

[41] Ibid.

[42] Ibid., p. 80.

[43] Cassius Dio Cocceianus, *Dio's Rome*, trans. Herbert B. Foster, 6 vols. (Troy, New York, 1906), III, 318-319, bk. 51.

[44] Ibid., p. 322.

⁴⁵Ibid., p. 323.

⁴⁶Plutarch, p. 79.

⁴⁷Dio Cassius, pp. 323-324.

⁴⁸Ibid., p. 327.

⁴⁹Ibid., p. 357

⁵⁰Plutarch, p. 86.

⁴¹Lucius Annaeus Florus, *Epitome of Roman History*, trans. Edward S. Forster (London, 1929), II, xxi.

⁵²I i 51-52.

⁵³I i 68-69.

⁵⁴I ii 91.

⁵⁵I ii 80-84.

⁵⁶I ii 33-38, 45-52, 119-126.

⁵⁷I ii 155.

⁵⁸I ii 183-193.

⁵⁹I ii 193-197.

⁶⁰II iii 19-26.

⁶¹II iii 72-74.

⁶²II iii 105.

⁶³III i 63.

⁶⁴III ii 5.

⁶⁵III ii 25.

⁶⁶III ii 57-58.

⁶⁷III ii 70-71.

⁶⁸III ii 73-74.

⁶⁹III ii 75-77.

⁷⁰IV i 27.

⁷¹IV i 28.

[72] IV i 63.

[73] IV i 80-81.

[74] IV i 166-167.

[75] IV i 181.

[76] IV i 203-205.

[77] Ellis-Fermor, p. 1.

[78] IV iv 1.

[79] IV i 51.

[80] IV i 59-61.

[81] V iii 1-3.

[82] V iii 7-9.

[83] V iii 84-85.

[84] V iii 109.

[85] V III 117.

[86] IV i 107.

[87] IV iv 84.

[88] IV iv 87-90.

[89] III ii 63-64.

[90] IV i 107-108.

[91] IV i 198.

[92] III i 1-31.

[93] I i 3.

[94] I i 93.

[95] I i 113.

[96] I ii 70-74.

[97] I ii 127.

[98] I ii 162-163.

[99] I ii 166-171.

[100] I ii 183-192.

[101] I ii 193-197

[102] I ii 199-204.

[103] II i 102-114.

[104] II i 112.

[105] II iii 107.

[106] III i 6-7.

[107] III i 18.

[108] V v 5-7.

[109] I i 105-107.

[110] V iii 48-50.

[111] IV i 20-28.

[112] II iv 113-116.

[113] John Webster, The Duchess of Malfi, in The Complete Works of John Webster, ed. F. L. Lucas, 4 vols. (London, 1927), II, 87.

[114] John F. Danby, Poets on Fortune's Hill (London, 1952), p. 168.

[115] L. G. Salingar, "The Decline of Tragedy," The Age of Shakespeare, in A Guide to English Literature, 7 vols. (Penguin Books, 1955), II, 438.

[116] G. F. Sensebaugh, The Tragic Muse of John Ford (Stanford, 1944), p. 23.

[117] Agrippina, I 137-141.

[118] Plutarch, p. 58.

[119] Ellis-Fermor, p. 20.

[120] Plutarch, p. 76.

[121] Daniel, p. 62, ll. 844-849.

[122] L. C. Knights, Drama and Society in the Age of Jonson (London, 1951), p. 154.

[123] I i 89-90.

[124] V ii 70.

[125] V ii 63.

[126] V i 5-6.

[127] Chester, p. 76ff, p. 131ff, p. 172ff.

[128] Salingar, P. 430.

[129] Danby, p. 181.

[130] G. M. Trevelyan, The Tudors and the Stuart Era, in History of England, 3 vols. (Garden City, N.Y., 1954), II, 153.

[131] Ibid., p. 166.

[132] Ibid., pp. 157-158.

[133] Danby, p. 165.

[134] Ibid., p. 161.

[135] Ibid., p. 167.

[136] Ibid., p. 163.

[137] Ibid., p. 186.

[138] Ibid., pp. 179-180.

[139] I i 1-2.

[140] I i 3.

[141] I i 5-6.

[142] I i 6-7.

[143] I i 7-8.

[144] Florus, II, xxi.

[145] Louis B. Wright, ed., Advice to a Son: Precepts of Lord Burghley, Sir Walter Raleigh, and Francis Osborne (Ithaca, N.Y., 1962), p. 1, 7.

[146] Ibid., p. xxi.

[147] Ibid., p. xxiii.

[148] Ibid., p. xviii, xx, xxiv.

[149] Ibid., p. xxv.

[150] Ibid., p. 9.

[151] Ibid., p. 10.

[152] Ibid., p. 21.

[153] Ibid., pp. 21-22.

[154] Ibid., p. xxiii.

[155] Ibid., p. xxvi.

[156] Ibid., p. 63.

[157] Ibid., pp. 69-70.

[158] Ibid., p. 69.

[159] Ibid., n.

[160] Ibid., p. 69.

[161] The ms title page claims the play was acted in 1626 and Chester believes it to be the date of both composition and acting (p. 98). The play is not listed in Mary S. Steele, Plays and Masques at Court (New Haven, 1926). Bentley argues for a public performance (Jacobean Stage, IV, 835).

[162] Wright, p. xxv.

[163] Hyder E. Rollins and Herschel Baker, eds., The Renaissance in England: Non-Dramatic Prose and Verse of the Sixteenth Century (Boston, 1954), p. 422.

[164] John Harington, Nugæ Antiquæ, ed. Henry Harington, 2 vols. (London, 1804), I, 352.

[165] Ibid., p. 350.

[166] Ibid., pp. 350-351.

[167] Ibid., pp. 392-396.

[168] The Autobiography of Edward, Lord Herbert of Cherbury, ed. Sidney L. Lee (London, 1886), pp. 86-87.

[169] Sensebaugh, p. 140.

[170] Ibid., p. 105.

[171]Danby, p. 163.

[172]Salinger, p. 431.

[173]Danby, p. 170.

[174]Sensebaugh, p. 96.

[175]*Ibid.*, p. 106.

[176]*Ibid.*

[177]*Ibid.*, p. 108.

[178]Ibid., pp. 109-112.

[179]Daniel, p. 94, ll. 1766-1771.

The Tragœdy of Cleopatra

Queene of Aegypt.

The speakers.

Antoniani.	Aegyptii.	Caesarei.
Marcus Antonius.	Cleopatra.	Cæsar Augustus.
Marcus Titius.	Eira.	Marcus Agrippa.
Munatius Plancus.	Charmio.	Cornelius Gallus.
C: Canidius Crassus.	Achoreus.	Pinnarius Scarpus.
Caius Sossius.	Euphronius.	Proculeius.
Titus Domitius.	Seleucus.	Thyreus.
Lucilius.	Glaucus.	Epaphroditus.
Aristocrates.	Mardio.	

Acted 1626.

The Scene Aegypt.

----------------------quantum impulit Argos
Iliacasque domos facie Spartana nocenti,
Hesperios auxit tantum Cleopatra furores.

                                            Luc:

[Act I, Scene 1]

Titius, Plancus, Canidius.

<u>Ti</u>.   Shame and dishonour to the Roman name!
A triumph held at Alexandria
Only to honour <u>Cleopatraes</u> pride!

<u>Pla</u>.   Ah <u>Marcus</u>, this Aegyptian Queene was made
To bee the ruine of <u>Antonius</u>.

<u>Ca</u>.   To bee the pleasure of <u>Antonius</u>.

<u>Pla</u>.   How can you jest, <u>Canidius</u>, on a theame
So sadd?

<u>Ca</u>.   How <u>Plancus</u> can you prophecy
So saddly on so merry an occasion
As is the love of Ladyes?

<u>Ti</u>.   Lett <u>Canidius</u>   10
Have his owne way, <u>Munatius</u>, 'tis in vaine
To talke to him.

<u>Ca</u>.   Would you could lett mee have
<u>Antonius</u> his way, upon condition
I suffred you to censure gravely of it.
And prophecy my ruine. But, my Lords,
You were as good bee merry too, and take
Youre share of pleasures in th' Aegyptian Court.

15 Lords,] 1639; frends ms

You'll doo no good with these persuasions.
Hee loves the Queene, and will doo so in spite
Of oure morality.

<u>Pla</u>.   Tis too too true,   20
That face of hers, that beauty in the budd,
Now fully blowne, in years of innocence
(If any years of hers were innocent)
Sett off with no adulterismes of Art,
Nor cloath'd with state, and pompous majesty:
But in a fortune clouded and distrest,
A wretched prisoner in her brothers Court,
Yett then I say that charming face could moove
The manly temper of wise <u>Julius Cæsar</u>.
That Mars in heat of all his active warre   30
When hee pursu'd the flying <u>Pompey</u> hither,
His sword yett reeking in Pharsaliaes slaughter
At sight of her became a doating lover;
And could wee thinke that oure <u>Antonius</u>
A man not master of that temperance
That <u>Cæsar</u> had, could finde a strength to guard
His soule against that beauty, now sett off
With so much wealth and Majesty?

20   Tis...true,] 1639; tis like enough. ms
27   Court] 1639; house ms

Ca.   No surely:

I did not thinke Antonius was an Eunuch.

Nor could I have beleev'd hee had beene worthy   40

To bee a successour in Cæsar's power

Unlesse hee had succeeded him in her.

Great Julius noble acts in warre and state

Assur'd the world that hee was wise and valiant:

But if hee had not fall'n in love with her

I should have much suspected his good nature.

Ti.   Nay then, Canidius, it must bee yours.

Ca.   Or what indeed were greatnesse in the world

If hee that did possesse it might not play

The wanton with it? This Aegyptian Queene   50

Is a state-beauty, and ordain'd by fate

To bee possest by them that rule the world.

Great Pompey's Sonne enjoy'd her first, and   Plutarch
                                         pluck'd   in Anton.

Her virgin blossome. When that family

Whose ruines fill'd the world, was overthrowne,

Great Julius next came in as Conquerour

To have his share, and, as hee did in power,

Succeeded him in Cleopatraes love.

Now oure Antonius takes his turne, and thinkes

That all the legions, all the swords that came   60
To make his greatnesse upp, when <u>Julius</u> dy'd,
Could give no greater priviledge to him
Then power to bee the Servant to this Queene.
Thus whoosoere in Rome bee Conquerour
His laurell wreath is <u>Cleopatraes</u> love.
And to speake justly of her, Nature seem'd
To build this woman for no meaner height.
Her Soule is full of greatnesse, and her witt
Has charms as many as her beauty has.
With Majesty beyond her sexe shee rules   70
Her spatious kingdome, and all neighbour-Princes
Admire her parts. How many languages
Speakes shee with elegance! Embassadors
From th' Aethiopians, Arabs, Troglodites,   <u>Plutarch</u>.
From th' Hebrews, Syrians, Medes, and Parthians
Have in amazement heard this learned Queene
Without the aide of an interpreter
In all theire severall tongues returne them answers,
When most of her dull predecessour kings
Since <u>Ptolemæus Philadelphus</u> time   80
Scarse understood th' Aegyptian tongue, and some

67   this⌋1639; that ms

Had quite forgott the Macedonian.

Ti.   How well Canidius descants on this theame!

Pla. I'll lay my life it pleases him; the man
Is deepe in love, and pity tis hee has
So great a rivall as Antonius.

Ca.   Well use youre witts upon mee. But I doubt
If any man could search youre secrett thoughts,
Tis envy not morality that makes
You taxe his love, how gravely ere you talke.   90

Ti.   But can Canidius thinke it should bee just
In oure Antonius to forsake for her
His lawfull wife the good Octavia?

Ca.   Then like a Roman lett mee answer, Marcus.
Is it become a care worthy of us
What woman Antony enjoyes? Have wee
Time to dispute his matrimoniall faults
That have already seene the breach of all
Romes sacred lawes, by which the world was bound?
Have wee endur'd oure Consuls state and power   100
To bee subjected by the lawlesse armes
Of private men, oure Senatours proscrib'd,
And can wee now consider whither they

That did all this, may keepe a wench or no?

It was the crime of us and fate it selfe

That <u>Antony</u> and <u>Cæsar</u> could usurpe

A power so great, beyond which wee can suffer

No more worth thinking of; nor were't to us

Any great fortune of <u>Antonius</u>

Were honest of his body.

<u>Pla</u>.   Have wee then,   110

Whoo have beene greatest Magistrates, quite lost

All show of liberty, and now not dare

To counsell him?

<u>Ca</u>.   A show of liberty

When wee have lost the substance, is best kept

By seeming not to understand those faults

Which wee want power to mend. For mine owne part

I love the person of <u>Antonius</u>,

And through his greatest loosenesse can discerne

A nature freeer, honester then <u>Cæsar's</u>.

And if a warre do grow twixt them, (as surely   120

Ambition would ere long find out a cause

Although <u>Octavia</u> had not beene neglected)

Rather then Rome should still obey two Lords

```
120    do]1639; should ms
123    still obey]1639; ever serve ms
```

Could wish that all were Antony's alone.

Whoo would, I thinke, bee brought more easily

Then Cæsar, to resigne the governement.

Pla.   Would I could thinke that either would doo so.

Here comes her servant Mardio.

                Enter Mardio.

Mar.   Noble Lords,

The Queen by mee entreats youre company

At supper with the Lord Antonius.   130

Ca.   Mardio, returne oure humble services

Wee'll instantly attend her. Now my friends   Exit
[Mardio.]
Can you a while putt off austerity

And rigid censures to bee freely merry?

Ti.   It may bee so. Wee'll try what wine can doo.   Exeunt.

      [Act I, Scene ii]

A Feast preparing. Euphronius, Glaucus, Charmio.

Eup.   Glaucus lett more of this perfume bee gott.

Gla.   I have enough in readynesse; or else

Twould bee too late to thinke on't now; the Queene

```
128  Here...Lords,]   1639; om. ms
129  The...mee]   1639; My Lords, the Queene ms
132  friends, ]   1639; Masters ms
135  try]  1639; see ms
s.d. A Feast preparing. ]   1639; om. ms
```

Is upon entrance.

Eup.   Charmio art thou sure
These tapers stand just as the Queene commanded?

Ch.   Tis the same order that Antonius
When last hee feasted heere, so much admir'd,
And saide 'mongst all the curiosityes   Plutarch.
That hee had seene, the placing of those lights
Did not the least affect him.

Eup.   Though the Romans   10
In power and warrelike state exceede us farre,
Yett in oure Court of Aegypt they may learne
Pleasure and bravery. But art thou sure
That all things here are well?

Ch.   As exquisite
As the Queens wish would have it. Hark they come.

  A flourish. Achoreus the Preist, Antonius, Cleopatra,
           Canidius, Titius, Plancus.

Cle.   To say, my Lord, that you are welcome hither
Were to disparage you, whoo have the power
To make youre selfe so; for what ere you see
In Aegypt is youre owne.

An.   What Aegypt holds
13 But art thou sure] 1639; But hearke they come. ms
14-15 That...come.] 1639; om. ms

> If I bee Judge, not all the world besides 20
> Can æ qualize.

Cle.   My Lord, will't please you take
Youre place, and these youre noble Roman frends?

An.   Father Achoreus, sitt you neere to mee.
Youre holy orders and great age, which shewes
The Godds have lov'd you well, may justly challenge
A reverence from us.

Cle.   Great Julius Cæsar
Did love my father well; hee oft was pleas'd
At howers of leisure to conferre with him
About the nature of oure Nile, of all
The mysteryes of religion, and the wonders 30
That Aegypt breedes.

Acho.   Hee had a knowing soule,
And was a master of philosophy
As well as warre.

An.   How like the splangled sky
These tapers make the high-arch'd roofe to shew!
While Cleopatra like bright Cynthia
In her full orbe more guilds the cheerfull night.
Shee's still at full; yett still meethinkes shee wexes,
And growes more faire and more Majesticall.

Cle. My lords, you Romans, whose victorious armes
Have made you masters of the world, possesse 40
Such full and high delights in Italy

That oure poore Aegypt can present no pleasure
Worth youre acceptance. But lett mee entreat
You would bee freely merry, and forgive
Youre entertainement.

An.   Tis an entertainment
That might invite and please the Godds. Meethinkes
<u>Jove</u> should descend, while <u>Cleopatra's</u> here,
Disguis'd for love, as once for feare hee was
When bold Typhœus scal'd the starry sky,
And all the Godds disguis'd in Aegypt lurk'd.   50
Love were a nobler cause then feare to bring him,
And such a love as thine.

Cle.   If I could thinke
That ere great <u>Jove</u> did play such prankes as those,
I'd now believe that hee were here disguis'd,
And tooke the noble shape of <u>Antony</u>.

An.   This complement so farre transcends, it leaves
No answere for a wit so dull as mine.

                    A Song.

<u>Not hee that knowes how to accquire</u>
<u>But to enjoy is blest</u>.
<u>Nor dooes oure happinesse consist</u>   60
<u>In motion but in rest</u>.

<u>The Godds passe man in blisse, because</u>
<u>They toile not for more height</u>;

57   a wit so dull]1639; so dull a braine ms

        But can enjoy, and in theire owne
        Eternall rest delight.

        Then Princes doo not toile, nor care.
        Enjoy what you possesse.
        Which whilest you doo, you æquallize
        The Godds in happinesse.

Ti.   Munatius Plancus, I was thinking now   [Aside.]   70
How Hannibal was charm'd at Capua,
When that delicious place had mollify'd
His rough and cruell soule and made him learne
The lessons of soft love and luxury.

Pla.   There was no cause, Marcus, for such a thought
For oure Antonius in the heat of all
His active life knew how to revell well.

An.   Lett this soft Musike cease, and louder sound.
The second course is mine. Call in Lucilius.

        Enter Lucilius with 3 crownes.

Faire Cleopatra for addition   80
To what thou hold'st the world-commanding Rome
Presents these crownes, and by my hand invests
Thee, Cleopatra, Queene of wealthy Cyprus,   Plutarch.
Of Cœlosyria and Phœnicia.
Blush not my love, nor lett Romes bounty force
Thy modesty. These crownes from thy faire brow
Receive more lusrre then they can bestow.

Ti.	I thinke hee needs not greatly feare her blushing.	[Aside.]

Pla.   No Marcus no. Alas these petty kingdomes
  (Though too too great to bee so ill bestow'd)   90
  Are not the scope of her ambitious aimes.

Cle.   My Lord, I dare not make excuse, or plead
  Unworthinesse where once Antonius wisedome
  Has made election to conferre his favours.

An.   Admire not frends; the goddlike power of Rome
  Is more declar'd by what it gives away   Plutarch.
  Then what it holds. But these are still oure owne,
  And Cleopatra Romes deserving frend.

Ca.   I cannot chuse but thinke how fitt a state
  For Cleopatra Cyprus kingdome is.   100
  And shall beleeve that it was ominous
  That noble Julius Cæsar after all
  Those fower rich triumphs which hee held at Rome
  When hee resolv'd with like magnificence
  To build a temple to the Goddesse Venus,
  From whome his house derive theire pedegree,
  Within his stately temple, to expresse
  The image of that Goddesse, hee sett upp
  Faire Cleopatraes figure in the place,
  Supposing her to bee the Queene of love.   110
  You know, my Lord Antonius, this is true.
  And Cyprus ever was faire Venus Ile.

An.   Twas well observ'd noble Canidius.

Ca.   Fill mee some wine! Health to the Cyprian Queene.

An. Drinke it to mee <u>Canidius</u>, and I thanke thee.
Lett it goe round, my frends.

Cle. I ever thought
My selfe much bound to brave <u>Canidius</u>
Since I was happy in his company.

An. How fitt it is! No other Cyprian Queene
But <u>Cleopatra</u> shall the Poëts know;   120
Whose fancyes shall advance that kingdome higher.
More amorous now will Paphos mountaines show,
And all those flowery Meades, the feilds of Love,
Ore which no windes but Westerne ever blow.
The aire it selfe will yeild a sweeter breath
While <u>Cleopatra</u> reignes the Cyprian Queene.

Pla. How amorous in his language hee is growne! [<u>Aside</u>.]
The times, I feare <u>Munatius</u> will require
A rougher language shortly, Wee shall heare
As soone as any newes can come from Rome.   130

An. But Long agoe was I enforc'd to know
That <u>Cleopatra</u> was the Queene of Love,   <u>Plutarch</u>.
When first I mett thee in Cilicia,
And downe the silver streame of Cidnus, thou
In Venus shape cam'st sailing, while the aire
Was ravish'd with thy Musicke, and the windes
In amorous gales did kisse thy silken sailes.
Thy maides in Graces habitts did attend,
And boys, like Cupids, painted quivers bore,

    While thousand Cupids in those starry eyes   140
    Stood ready drawne to wound the stoutest hearts.

<u>Cle</u>.   You came like <u>Mars</u> himself in threatning arms
    To ruine mee and my poore countrey then.
    I tooke that shape because I knew no strength,
    No power on earth was able to resist
    The conquering fury of <u>Antonius</u>.

<u>An</u>.   That face of thine resisted mee, and did
    So sweetly conquer, I was proud to yeild,
    And more rejoic'd in that captivity
    Then any Roman in a triumph did.   150

              <u>Enter</u> Hipparchus.

How now what newes with thee?

<u>Hip</u>.   Letters from Rome, my Lord.

<u>An</u>.   From whome?

<u>Hip</u>.   <u>Geminius</u>.

<u>An</u>.   Tomorrow wee'll peruse them. No affaires
    Of what import or height so ere, shall have
    Power to disturbe the pleasures of this night.
    Oure theame to night is love, which oft has made
    The thunderer himselfe a while lay be
    The weary burden of his governement.
    Come lead away.

<u>Ti</u>.   Twere fitt to read them now.
    None knowes what gaine a little time may bee.   160

An.   You may peruse them Titius; lead away.   Exeunt.

                        Manent Titius, Plancus.

Ti.   Can no affaires of what import so ere

  Breake one nights pleasure? Well Antonius,

  The tottring state thou holdst, must bee supported

  By nobler vertues, or it cannot stand.

Pla.   Cyprus, Phœnice, Cœlosyria

  Three wealthy kingdomes gott with Roman blood,

  And oure forefathers valour, giv'n away

  As the base hire of an adulterous bedd?

  Was Cyprus conquer'd by the sober vertue

  Of Marcus Cato to bee thus bestow'd?

Ti.   This act will please young Cæsar.

Pla.   Twill displease

  The Senate, Plancus, and Antonius frends.

Ti.   Alas, hee knowes not what true frendshipp meanes,

  But makes his frends his slaves, and which is worse

  Slaves to his lusts and vices. Could hee else

  Slight oure advise so? Men, whome Rome has seene

  Wearing her highest honours, and of birth

  As great as his. Unlesse hee change his minde

  I shall beleeve my frendshipp was ill plac'd

  And strive to place it better.

172 Ti...Pla.] 1639; om....Ti. ms
174 Ti.] 1639; Pla. ms

Pla. This last act

Will quickly bee at Rome.

Ti. They have enough

Already, noble Plancus; thinke you not

It will bee censur'd that the Roman name

Was much dishonour'd by that base surprise

Of Artavasdes the Armenian king?   Dio. Cass.

Whome through the streetes of Alexandria   Plutarch.

Hee ledd in triumph bound with golden chaines

Forcing the captive king (if all his threats

Could have enforc'd so much) prostrate t' adore   190

Proud Cleopatra, as if all his acts

And all the honour of his arms were due

To her and not to Rome. Calvisius too

In Senate late accus'd him for bestowing   Plutarch.

On Cleopatra that so farre renown'd

And famous library of Pergamus,

In which there were two hundred thousand bookes.

How many such wilde actions have her charmes

Enforc'd his weakenesse to?

Pla. His testament,

Which now at Rome the Vestall virgins keepe,   200

Of which wee two are privy to the sealing

Should it bee knowne, would stirre all Romans hate,

```
181  Pla. ] 1639; Ti. ms
182  Ti. ] 1639; Pla. ms
183  Plancus ] 1639; Titius ms.
199  Pla. ] 1639; Ti. ms
```

Willing his body, though hee dy'd at Rome,　　　　Dio.
To bee enter'd at Alexandria.　　　　　　　　Plutarch.
But if a warre twixt him and Cæsar grow
(As needes it must, although not yett declar'd)
For Cæsar now is levying men and money
Through Italy, Spaine, France, and Germany;
Against what foe can his designe bee bent
But oure Antonius? If a warre I say　　　　　　　　　　210
Twixt them should happen, tell mee noble Titius,
What should wee doo?

Ti.　　　　　　　　　　Fight for Antonius.

Pla.　　True, frend, were hee himselfe, or were there hope
Or possibility hee could bee so.
But shall oure valour toile in sweat and blood
Only to gaine a Roman Monarchy
For Cleopatra and th' effeminate rout
Of base Canopus? Shall her timbrells fright
Romes Capitoll, and her advanced pride
Tread on the necks of captive Senatours?　　　　　　　　220
Or, which is more, shall th' earths Imperiall seat
Remoove from Rome to Aegypts swarthy sands?
For whoo can tell if mad Antonius
Have promis'd her, as Caius Marius once
Promis'd the Samnites, to transferre the State?

```
205  Speech prefix om. ] 1639; Pla. ms
217  th' effeminate ] 1639; the vicious ms
223  if mad ] 1639; whither ms
```

Ti. It may bee so; his dotage is enough

To grant it her; her pride enough to aske it.

Munatius Plancus in this whole discourse

Thou speak'st my very thoughts. No more, here comes.

    Enter Lucilius.

Lucilius. Whither so fast?

Lu.   My Lords,   230

Downe to the Port to wait upon the Consuls.

The Roman Consuls both Titus Domitius

And Caius Sossius are from Rome arriv'd Dio.
              Suetonius.
Here at Pelusium. What the matter is

Is not yett knowne.

Pla.   Wee'll goe along with thee.

This now beginns to looke like businesse Marcus. Exeunt.

    Actus Secundus [Sc. i]

  Antonius, Sossius, Domitius, Canidius,

    Titius, Plancus, Ventidius.

An. Tis not the place, nor marble walls that make

A Senate lawfull, or decrees of power,

But convocation of the men themselves

The sacred order by true magistrates.

s.d. Ventidius] 1639; om. ms

2 power,] 1639; right: ms

Then Rome is heere. Here both her Consuls are.
Here are her Axes and her Fasces borne;
And no small number of that sacred order
Are here assisting. When the barbarous Gaules
Had taken Rome, when all the Senate fledd,
And with <u>Camillus</u> theire Dictator then   10
At Veii liv'd, Rome then at Veii was
As now in Aegypt. Fathers know the face
Of youre assembly; know youre lawfull power.
Consult, decree, and act what ere may bee
Happy and prosperous for the commonwealth.

<u>Sos</u>. Whilst power of lawes, whilest reverence of the
                                                Senate,
And due respect t' a Consul's dignity
Could give protection to the Consuls persons
Wee did maintaine thy cause, <u>Antonius</u>,
Against proud <u>Cæsar's</u> faction. Now since lawes   20
Are putt to silence, and the Senate forc'd,
The Consuls sacred priviledge infring'd
By rage and lawlesse armes, wee are expell'd,
And suffer banishment, to bee restor'd
And reindeniz'd by thy conquering sword.
Now justly draw it. Fate approves thy cause,
And on thy conquest setts a glorious price,
Greater then all thy former warrs could give.

15 for] 1639; to ms

Sextus Pompeius, Marcus Lepidus
Are ruin'd both, and all competitors   30
Are tane away; Fortune has left but one
To share the world with thee. Nor canst thou share
The world with him. His pride would barre thy right,
And Cæsar's glory dimme Antonius light.
Thou canst not shine unlesse alone thou shine.
Or all the world, or nothing must bee thine.

Dom.   The Consulshipp, which was design'd to thee,
The Senate have revoked, and decree   Dio.
Gainst Cleopatra warre, but mean it 'gainst thee.
What would theire malice dare, Antonius   40
Had fortune frown'd, thy kings and Provinces
Fall'n from obedience, that dare now provoke
Thy growing fortunes and assisting Godds?
Theire injury has made thy quarrell just.
Bee speedy then, and loose no time of action.

Sos.   Cæsar is needy. His Italian souldiers
Are apt to muteny for want of pay,   Dio.
                                                 Plutarch.
And might with ease bee tempted to revolt.

Ca.   Wee neede them not: oure strengths are greater farre
Then Cæsar's are; oure preparations readyer.   50
Nought but delay can question oure successe.
Shall wee decree the warre?

31 Are tane away] 1639; Remooved else ms
47 want] 1639; warre ms

An.   Stay noble Romans,
Before wee publish a decree, or shew
The reason of oure arms so justly tane,
Weigh but with mee the meanes and strength wee have.
Know, worthy frends, it is no desperate warre
Youre valours are engag'd in. Breifly thus.
Oure Roman strength is nineteene legions.
Ten kings in person will attend oure campe,
The kings of Affricke, Comegena, Thrace,   60
Upper Cilicia, Paphlagonia,   Plutarch.
Of Cappadocia, Pontus, Palaestine,
Of rich Arabia, and Galatia.
Oure strength at sea five hundred fighting shipps,
Well rigg'd and man'd; oure treasuryes are full;
And twenty thousand talents too the warre
Dooes **Cleopatra** freely contribute.
Why speake I more? The crowne of all my strength
Youre loves and spiritts are. The injuryes
On Which wee ground oure just and lawfull warre   70
Are breifely these. **Caesar** unjustly holds
These Provinces and armyes all that late
Belong'd to **Pompey** and to **Lepidus**   **Dio.**
                                                  Plutarch.
Refusing to divide them, or deliver
That Moity which appertaines to mee
Though oft demanded by my frends at Rome,
And letters from my selfe. Besides hee levyes

Both men and money ore all Italy, <u>Dio</u>.
<u>Plutarch</u>.
Which countrey, as you know, by oure agreement

Belongs to both, and should bee held in common. 80

<u>Sos</u>.   Most true.

<u>Ca</u>.   These wrongs are past all sufferance;

Thy warre is but defensive to regaine

Thine owne unjustly taken.

<u>Dom</u>.   The warre's just.

<u>Sos</u>.   And <u>Cæsar</u> the beginner of these broiles

From whome the wrong first sprung, most justly may

Bee judg'd an enemy to the peace of Rome.

<u>An</u>.   If fortune aide us in a cause so just,

And wee returne victorious, noble Romans,

I make a vow, and lett it bee recorded,

Within two moneths after the warre is ended 90

I will lay downe the governement I hold,   <u>Dio</u>.

And freely then resigne my power againe

Unto the Senate and the people of Rome.

<u>Sos</u>.   Lett it bee sixe moneths rather; for two moneths

Will bee too short a time to settle it.

<u>Dom</u>.   <u>Sossius</u> speakes well, my Lord.   <u>Dio</u>.

<u>An</u>.   Lett it bee so.

And all the Godds assist mee as I meane

A just and true performance.

<u>Ca</u>.   All the Godds

Preserve <u>Antonius</u> father of his countrey.

<u>Om</u>.   Author and champion of oure liberty.   <u>Exeunt</u>. 100

Manent Titius, Plancus.

Ti. Lett them beleeve that list, for mee I thinke
The resignation of a power so great
Will bee a termperance too great for him
Ere to expresse.

Pla. Or if hee would, hee must
Aske leave of <u>Cleopatra</u>, and her pride
Will hardly grant him that.

Ti. Nor will I fight
To make her Mistres of the world and him.
Have you consider'd noble frend, of what
Wee lately spake?

Pla. And am resolved, <u>Marcus</u>
The frends and followers wee shall bring with us   110
Will make us welcome guests to <u>Cæsar's</u> side.
It seemes the City favours <u>Cæsar</u> much
That both the Consuls fledd from Rome for feare.
Nor is oure action base. The scornes and wrongs
Wee have endur'd at <u>Cleopatraes</u> hands   <u>Plutarch.</u>
                                                                                             <u>Dio.</u>
Would tempt a moile to fury; and both sides
Stand aequall yett.

Ti. Come lett's away, tis time.

Pla. Aegypt farewell.

Ti. Farewell <u>Antonius</u>   <u>Exeunt</u>

111   guests] 1639; frends ms
112   City favours] 1639; Senate favour   ms

[Act II, Sc. ii]

Seleucus, Glaucus.

Se. How suddainly the scene is changed here
From love and banquetts to the rough alarms
And threatning noise of warre!
Gla.   The change, Seleucus,
Is not so suddaine as you speake; this storme
Has beene expected long. The two great Lords
Of all the Roman world Antonius
And Cæsar have in heart beene enemyes
These many years; and every man has wonder'd
'T has beene withheld so long, considering
How much complaining has beene daily made   10
By them, theire frends and factions 'gainst each other.
Whose cause is justest lett the Godds determine.
Se. No other justice then ambition
Makes them to draw theire swords; no other cause
Then that the world cannot endure two Sunns.
Gla. The thing that troubles mee, Seleucus, is
I heare it spoken in the Court, the Queene
Her selfe in person will associate
Antonius to the warre.
Se.   I heare that rumour.
But hope it is not true. How nakedly,   20

And in what great confusion would this land
Bee left! And what addition can her person
Among so many Roman legions
Bring to <u>Antonius</u>?

<u>Gla</u>.   Lett us enquire
 The certainty; I faine would bee resolv'd.

<u>Se</u>. I on necessity must know, before
 The Queene can goe, that order may bee taken
 About the fort I keepe, what strength shee meanes
 To leave within it in her absence.

<u>Gla</u>.   True,
 That reason will excuse thee for enquiring.   <u>Exeunt</u>.   30

[Act II, Sc. iii]

               Cleopatra, Canidius.

<u>Cle</u>. Noble <u>Canidius</u>, I'll enstruct no more,
 Nor use moe circumstances, for I know
 To whome I have referr'd my businesse,
 And trust youre wisedome.

<u>Ca</u>.   Royall <u>Cleopatra</u>,
 I am so fortify'd with reasons now   <u>Plutarch</u>.
 That maugre <u>Sossius</u> and <u>Domitius</u>
 With all theire best persuasions, I'll prevaile;
 You shall not stay behinde; feare it not Madam.

Cle.   Brave Roman, weare this jewell for my sake;

And bee possest of Cleopatraes love.   10

Second my suit; there lyes not in my power

A thing to grant I should deny Canidius.

Ca.   The favours, Madam, you can give, have power

T' obleige the greatest Monarchs of the world.

Cle.   Bee ready, worthy frend, hee'll straight bee here.
                                                    Exit Can.
None but Canidius has the power to worke

Antonius in this action, which the rest

Will all oppose I know, a thing on which

My state, my hopes and fortunes all depend.

Hee must persuade Antonius to take   20

Mee with him to the warre; for it I stay

Behinde him here, I runne a desperate hazard;

For should Octavia enterpose herselfe

In this great warre (as once before shee did)

And make her brother, and her husband friends

Wher's Cleopatra then? But here he comes.

              Enter Antonius.

An.   Sweete Cleopatra, I should plead excuse

For leaving thee a while, but that the cause

Is of a nature so immense and high,

25 And...friends] 1639; And make them frends, that end
    to me were fatall. ms
26 Wher's...comes.] 1639; om. ms

    And brings effects of such advantage home 30
    That thou, I know, art pleas'd it should bee so.
    And with a patience canst resolve to beare
    So small an absence, that my wish'd returne
    May call thee mistres· of the subject world.

<u>Cle</u>.   Cannot <u>Antonius</u> then bee fortunate
  If <u>Cleopatra</u> goe? Is there in mee
  So badd an omen? Did I thinke there were
  Not for the world would I desire to beare
  You company, but rather dy at home .

<u>An</u>.   Farre are my thoughts from giving entertainement 40
  To such fond dreames; I would not venture thee.

<u>Cle</u>.   My life and fortunes both depend on yours;
  As much in Aegypt will my danger bee
  As in youre army, and my torment more,
  To dy each hower for feare, and to remaine
  In sadd suspence till messengers can bring
  The newes so farre. But if my company
  Distast my Lord, I cannot wish his greife.

<u>An</u>.   Can <u>Cleopatra</u> thinke her heavenly presence
  Can bee distastfull, or not valu'd more
  Then all joyes else? Parted from thee I thinke
  All places sadd, all lands disconsolate.
  Before this life I prize thy company;
  But must not have it now. Doo not entreat;
  I have deny'd it to my selfe already,

And in the Campe should bee asham'd to rise

From Cleopatraes armes, when warres rough noise

Shakes all the world, when kings and Senatours

Are venturing lives and fortunes in my service.

Oh stay behinde, and lett thy presence make   60

Aegypt a place, to which I would desire

If C<u>æsar's</u> fortune conquer, to retire.

<u>Cle</u>.   If that should happen (which the Godds avert)

What land, alas, could comfort mee? Or lend

A safe retreat to vanquish'd <u>Antony</u>?

Thou would'st disdaine to draw a wretched breath,

And I as much should scorne captivity.

But I had thought the Roman <u>Antony</u>

Had lov'd so great a Queene with noble love,

Not as the pleasure of his wanton bed   70

Or mistris only of some looser houres,

But as a partner in his highest cares,

And one whose soule hee thought were fitt to share

In all his dangers, all his deedes of honour.

Without that love I should disdain the other.

<u>An</u>.   Doo not mistake mee, noble Queene, I know

Thy breast is full of high Heroike worth.

68 Roman <u>Antony</u>] 1639; honourable Roman ms
70 Not...bed] 1639; Not as the mistresse of his looser
    thoughts, ms
71 Or...houres,] 1639; <u>om</u>. ms
75 Without...other.] 1639; <u>om</u>. ms
77 worth] 1639; thoughts ms

Cle. How can you thinke it so, that could so long

In times of peace and pleasure recreate

Youre selfe with mee in Aegypts Court: yett now   80

When honour calls reject my company?

An. I should desire it rather then my life;

But that my Roman frends are all against it.

    Enter Sossius, Domitius, Canidius.

See here they come; if they agree, 'tis done.

Now noble frends, on whose oraculous counsells

And matchlesse valour my whole fate depends,

Speake what you thinke; should Cleopatra goe

In person to the warre, or stay behinde?

Sos. I have deliver'd my opinion,

And so has my Colleague.

An.   What thinkes Canidius?   90

Ca. I thinke, my Lord, tis fitt the Queene, whose bounty

Has brought so great assistance to the warre

Should not bee left behinde. Besides, her presence

Will much encourage her Aegyptian souldiers,

Of whome a great part of the fleete consists.   Plutarch.

An. Tis true Canidius.

Cle.   Lett not my sexe

Disparage mee. For which of all those kings,

That now in person serve Antonius

Have more experience in affaires of weight

84 agree] 1639; consent ms
95 Plutarch.] 1639; om. ms

         Then I, my Lord, whoo have so long beene privy   100
         To youre high counsells? And in love to you
         And youre designes whoo should compare with mee?

An.   What thinke you frends? You heare <u>Canidius</u>.

<u>Dom</u>.   If you bee pleas'd, I will subscribe.

<u>Sos</u>.   And I,
         Since things goe so.

<u>Cle</u>.   My wishes are effected. [<u>Aside</u>.]

An.   <u>Titius</u> and <u>Plancus</u> are both fledd to <u>Cæsar</u>.

<u>Ca</u>.   You shall not neede theire helpe, my Lord, at all.

An.   Come, lett's away.

<u>Cle</u>.   My strengths are ready all,
         And waite but youre command.

An.   Spoke like <u>Bellona</u>.
         <u>Canidius</u>, returne you to youre charge,   <u>Plutarch</u>. 110
         And bring those sixteene cohorts down to sea.
         Meete mee at Samos with them; both the Consuls
         Shall goe along with mee. Great father <u>Mars</u>,
         And all you Godds, that from the skyes behold
         The Roman labours, whose propitious aide
         Advanc'd my fortunes to so great an height,
         Make perfect that, which you youre selves begunne.
         This is the swords last worke, the judging hower
         Of nations fates, of mine and <u>Cæsar's</u> power.
         On which the starrs, and destinyes attend,   120
         And all the fortunes of mankinde depend.   <u>Exeunt</u>.

[Act II, Sc. iv]

Achoreus.

Acho. What dire portents sent from the wrathfull Godds
Threaten th' astonish'd world? What plagues are those
Which in the skyes prodigious face I read?
Tumultuous Nature teemes with monstrous births
As if the throwes would breake her labouring wombe;
What ruine lesse then Chaos shall involve
The mourning face of Nature? What great fate,
What kinde of mischeife is it? O yee Godds
Why did you add to wretched men a care
So past theire strength to beare, to lett them know   10
By dire presages theire ensuing woe?
Unknowne and secret lett youre vengeance bee;
And none foresee theire following misery:
But hope as well as feare. Jove hide thy doomes;
Keepe shutt oh fates youre adamantine bookes.
Lett not the banefull curiosity
Of human knowledge search youre secrett counsells,
And read youre purposes, to nourish so
A killing feare before the danger grow.

    Enter Seleucus, Glaucus.

Se.   That Comet's gone.

Gla.   It moov'd directly upwards,   20
And did not vanish till it seem'd to reach   Dio.
The firmament.

Acho.   What talke you of my Sonns?

Gla.   That Comet, Father, ore the Graecian Sea.

Acho.   It was a strange one both for forme and greatnesse,
And bodes some mischeife whersoere it light.
The Godds avert it from oure Aegypts coast.

Se.   Pinnarius Scarpus has received newes
That Italy and Rome it selfe are fill'd
With prodigyes. An ugly owle of late   Dio.
Did fly into the house of Concord first,   30
Thence beeing driven away it pearch'd againe
Within the Temple of the peoples Genius.
There, though all striv'd, it neither could bee caught,
Nor driven away; but flew at leisure out.
A sacred trophee on mount Aventine,   Dio.
Victoriaes image on the theater
By suddaine tempests were throwne downe and broken.   Dio.

Gla.   In Rome and other parts of Italy
Suddaine and strangely kindled fires have done
Exceeding wast; and wee are certify'd   40
That now Sicilian Aetna nourishes   Dio.
More horrid flames then usually it dooes,
And farther casts his scorching entrailes forth,
Blasting the feilds, and burning upp the corne.

41   Dio.] 1639; om. ms

A two-legg'd dragon in Etruria
Full fourescore foot in length was lately seene,
Which after much annoyance of the countrey   Dio.
It selfe with lightning was consum'd at last.
But these portents doo threaten Italy.

Acho. Alas my sonns, there neede no prodigyes   50
To shew the certaine losse of Italy.
For on both sides doo Roman Eagles stand
And Rome must bleede whoo ere by conquerour.
Besides her liberty for ever lost
When this sadd feild is fought. But that's not all;
What clime so farre, what region so remote,
But that the Roman fortune reaches thither?
All nations share in this.

Gla.   What hast thou gott,
By all thy conquests Rome, by all the blood
Which thy ambition through the world has shedd,   60
But rais'd a power which now thou canst not rule,
Nourish'd a lion to devoure thy selfe?
Would none but Roman blood might quench the fire
Of Romes dissentions, and no land beside
Bee forc'd to pay the forfeit of theire pride.
With evill omen did Aeneas first
Transport the reliques of Troys fatall fire
To Italy, that kindled greater there
It might at last like lightning through the world

Rend every nation. Was it not enough 70
That first youre conquests strew'd the earth with slaughter,
And dy'd all regions with theire natives bloods,
But youre dissentions still must teare the world?

Acho.   I'll go within, and make an offering
   To great Osiris.   Exit Achoreus.
Se.   Well may it succeede.
Aegypt will flourish if Antonius conquer.

Gla.   If hee should fall, the fury of the warre
Would light on Aegypt most, and wee should rue
That ere Antonius lov'd this happlesse land.

            Enter Mardio.

Mar.   Oh gentlemen, the strangest newes, that ere 80
Was seene in Aegypt.

Gla.   What's that Mardio?

Mar.   Thousands of people with astonishment
And feare beheld it. On those fruitfull plaines
That Southward ly from Alexandria,
Where never raine was knowne to fall before
It rain'd whole showers of blood, whose colour sett   Dio.
A purple dy upon those verdant feilds;
And in the clouds that horrid noise was heard
That meeting armyes make, beating of drumms,
Shrill trumpetts sound, armour 'gainst armour clashing, 90
As if the blood that fell, dropt from the wounds   Dio.

74 I'll...within] 1639; I will goe in ms
91 Dio.] 1639; om. ms.

Those aery battells made.

Gla. This is more strange
Then all the rest. This is oure owne Seleucus.

Se. Well gentlemen, I'll to Pelusium
And fortify the towne, to keepe oure foes
If foes bee conquerours, from entring there.

Gla. Yes, and oure frends, if they bee vanquished.
Keepe out oure frends, Seleucus, if theire presence
May plucke a warre, and ruine on oure heads.

Se. As there's occasion wee'll determine that. 100

Enter Achoreus.

Acho. Avert youre anger, Godds, if all too late
Oure prayers come not now.

Gla. What is it father?
Youre lookes I see are full of ruth and woe.

Acho. Oh wretched Aegypt, oh unhappy land!
In what hast thou so stirr'd the wrath of heaven?
The greived Godd refus'd his offering   Dio.
Bellowing aloud that all the Temple rung,
And from his sacred eyes the teares rann downe.
Would I could contradict or not beleeve
The skill which surest observations teach. 110
This signifyes a change of government.

Gla. What heaven is pleas'd to send, wee must endure.

Acho. True sonne, and lett a wise man place his strengths

Within himselfe, not trust to outward aides,
That whatsoever from the Godds can come
May finde him ready to receive theire doome.   Exeunt.

Actus Tertius [Sc. 1]

Enter Pinnarius Scarpus with souldiers.

Pin.   'Tis not Antonius, worthy souldiers,
But Rome herselfe to whome you ow youre valours.
What hee could claime you have perform'd already.
And serv'd him truly, whilest hee was to you
A Generall, to Rome, a magistrate.
You are discharg'd from all obedience
You ow'd to him by fate it selfe, and may
Nay ought to follow him, whome Roman fates
Appoint youre Generall, the noble Cæsar
Great Julius heire, not to his name alone,
But spirit and fortunes, which have both appear'd
In this so great and finall a defeat
Given to Antonius. Before wee knew not
To whome the Godds and Fortune had assign'd
Pure service, souldiers; now they have declar'd;
And lett us follow where they please to lead.
For faith is impious striving to susteine
That side whose fall the Godds themselves ordaine.

Sol.   Cæsar, Cæsar, Cæsar.

Pin.   Youre judgements guide you right. For could you thinke   20
  So small a strength as ours could raise againe
  The desperate state of fall'n Antonius,
  Under whose ruine all those legions sunke?
  What maddnesse were it, souldiers, to preferre
  A hopelesse civill warre before the weale
  And peace of Rome, and desperately provoke
  The prosperous fortune of victorious Cæsar?
  I have already to Cornelius Gallus
  By letter signify'd oure purposes,   Dio.
  Whoo sent from Cæsar now is marching hither   30
  To joine his strength with ours. But hearke his drumme

                    Enter Gallus

  Gives notice of his comming.

Gall.   Haile, Pinnarius Scarpus.

Pin.   All haile Cornelius Gallus
  Most wish'd for, and most happily arriv'd
  At Paraetonium.

Gall.   Victorious Cæsar
  With Love and favour greetes Pinnarius Scarpus,
  Cæsar, then whome the world acknowledges
  No other power, whome Fortune now has made
  Sole lord of all.

Pin.   I and my souldiers   40

With Parætonium are at Cæsar's service.

Whither's Antonius fledd?

Gall.   Hither to Aegypt

With Cleopatra. Twas a victory

So strangely giv'n away, as not the like

In former times I thinke has ere been heard;

On which especially so great a price

As the sole sway of all the world depended.

The fleetes encountred both, while both the campes

On either shore stood to behold the fight.   Dio.

Here the Cæsarian, there th' Antonian fleete   50

With æquall hopes came on, with fury æquall,

And long maintain'd a sharpe and cruell fight

With mutuall slaughter, while the Oceans face

Was forc'd to loose his colour, and receive

A crimson dy. The shipps Antonius had

Were Tall, and slowly did like castles moove: Dio.
                                                Florus.
But Cæsar's small, yett quicke and active   Plutarch.
                             stirr'd
On every side with all advantages.

Long Fortune doubted, and bright victory

Knew not which way to leane, but kept them both   60

In æquall ballance, till Antonius

Himselfe at last betray'd his glorious hopes.

For when his mistresse Cleopatra fledd   Plutarch.
                                                Dio.
Although a while within his manly breast   Florus.

The Roman honour strove 'gainst wanton Love,

45   has ere been heard;] 1639; was ever heard. ms

Love gott the conquest, and <u>Antonius</u>

Fledd after her, leaving his souldiers there

To sell theire lives in vaine. Whoo many howers

Though hee were fledd, made good the navall fight.

And had <u>Antonius</u> stay'd, it might be fear'd 70

<u>Cæsar</u> had not prevail'd. At last the fleete

Wanting theire Admirall, though not without

Much slaughter, fledd, or yeilded all to <u>Cæsar</u>.

<u>Pin.</u>   But what became of all his strength at land?

<u>Gall.</u>   Nay there's the wonder; there's <u>Antonius</u> maddnesse,

And such a maddnesse as will strike amazement

To all that heare it told. After his flight

Hee nere return'd, though in the campe hee had

Under the conduct of <u>Canidius,</u>

And other Captaines nineteen legions 80

Fresh and unfought; which might with reason hope

Had hee beene there, to have recover'd all.

They still remain'd encamped, and though oft

Sollicited by <u>Caesar</u> to revolt

Were kept from yeilding by <u>Canidius</u>   <u>Plutarch</u>.

In hope of <u>Antony's</u> returne; untill

<u>Canidius</u> fearing his owne souldiers mindes

And <u>Cæsar's</u> anger, fledd away by night.

They then despairing yeilded all to <u>Cæsar</u>.

Whoo by this time, I thinke, 's arriv'd in Aegypt 90

About Pelusium.

Pin.   Will you veiw the towne?

Gall.   With all my heart noble Pinnarius.   Exeunt.

         [Act III, Sc. ii]

         Cæsar, Agrippa, Titius, Plancus,
         Thyreus, Epaphroditus, Proculeius.

Cæs.   Antonius then with Cleopatra's fledd
To Alexandria.

Agr.   Tis certaine, Caesar.

Pla.   They say the vanquish'd Queene most cunningly
(fearing it seemes to bee excluded else   Dio.
From her owne kingdome) fain'd her selfe victorious
Landing in Aegypt with triumphant songs
Her shipps all crown'd with laurell, to deceive
The credulous people. Where beeing entred once
Shee leaves unpractis'd no strange tyranny;
And, as wee heare, to winne the Parthian king   10
Unto her side, beheaded Artavasdes   Dio.
King of Armenia, and the Parthian's foe
Whoo was her prisoner, that Artavasdes,
Whome Antony so basely had surprised.

Ti.   Cæsar, twere fitt to take Pelusium
Before wee march to Alexandria.

Cæs.   Twas oure intent, good Titius, not to leave

17 intent, good   ] 1639; intention ms

A towne of that import behinde oure backes.

Go Proculeius, summon it, and know

Whither the Governour will yeild or no.　　　Exit　　　20
　　　　　　　　　　　　　　　　　　　　　　　　Proculeius.

　　　　　　　　Enter Servant.

What newes with thee?

Ser.　　　　　　　　　　Caesar, a messenger

From Cleopatra craves admittance.

Caes.　　　　　　　　　　　Bring him.

　　　　　　　　Enter Euphronius.

Eup.　　Queene Cleopatra to great Caesar wishes

All health and victory, and humbly proffers

Herselfe, and all her fortunes to his service.

In token of which shee here presents by mee　　　　　Dio.

This crowne and scepter.

Pla.　　　　　　　Brave and ominous.

Eup.　　Humbly entreating Caesar's noble favour

To her and hers. The rest of her desires

So please it Caesar to peruse the same,　　　　　　　　30

This letter holds.

Pla.　　　　　　　I warrant a love letter.

Caes.　　But tell mee first where is Antonius?

Eup.　　I'll truly tell (though it may seeme to some

Incredible) that great Antonius

34　that] 1639; the ms

A man of late in conversation
So free, and full of jollity, in a strange
Deepe melancholly has retir'd himselfe
To Pharos Ile. Where like Athenian <u>Timon</u>, <u>Plutarch</u>.
                  <u>Strabo</u>. <u>lib</u>. 17.
Whoo did professe a hatred to mankinde,
And fledd all company, hee lives alone;   40
And on the solitary shore has built
A little house to feede his frantike humour,
And imitate that <u>Timon's</u> life, whose name
Hee takes unto himself. No frends at all,
Nor servants are admitted to his presence
But only two, Roman <u>Lucilius</u>,
And <u>Aristocrates</u> the Græcian.

Cæs. Not <u>Cleopatra</u>? Then I doubt the man
Growes weary of these worldly vanityes.

Agr. I never heard of such a change as this.   50

Pla. To what extreames unconstant men are carry'd!

Cæs. Give mee the letter; I'll peruse it now. <u>Reades</u>.
<u>Agrippa</u>.

Agr. Cæsar!   <u>They retire</u>.

Cæs. Here the woman writes
That for her liberty, and to confirme
The crowne of Aegypt to herselfe and children
To gratify my favour, shee has hidd   <u>Dio</u>.
Within her Pallace a great masse of gold <u>Plutarch</u>.

53 s.d. <u>They retire</u>] 1639; <u>om</u>. ms
57 <u>Plutarch</u>.] 1639; <u>om</u>. ms

Unknowne t' Antonius.

Agr.   Tis like enough;
For Cleopatra's rich, and long has beene,
Besides the sacriledge shee lately did   60
In robbing all the Temples of the Godds
About these parts.

Cæs.   I would not loose this gold;
Nor willingly let Cleopatra dy
Before her person have adorn'd my triumph.

Agr.   That will bee hard to bring to passe, and must
Bee wrought with subtlety. You must not send
A threatning message backe. For if you doo,
All's lost, her life, her gold and all are vanish'd.
For Cleopatra, as in all her acts
It has appear'd, is of a wondrous spirit,   70
Of an ambition greater then her fortunes
Have ever beene, though shee so long have sway'd
A Soveraingnety ore halfe the Roman world,
Trodd on the necks of humbled kings, and rul'd
Antonius as her slave. Her haughty spirit
Will never stoope so much as to a thought
Of such captivity.

Cæs.   I doo not meane
To lett her know my minde, or once suspect
If I can helpe it. But I have it now.
Thyreus come hither. I must now rely   80

Upon thy wisedome, care, and diligence

In an employment that concernes mee nerely.

But I am confident. Goe with this fellow

To Alexandria; use to the Queene

Thy best and most persuasive oratory.   Dio.
                                                                            Plutarch.

Tell her I love her, and extremely dote

On her admired beauty. Thou art wise,

And need'st no great instructions. The successe

I doo not doubt; the woman's credulous,

And thinkes all men are bound to bee in love   90

With that ensnaring face. If thou perceive

Shee will be wrought on, winne her to betray

Antonius to my hand. The way to woo her

I leave good Thryeus to thy eloquence

And cunning working of it. Spare thy reply.

Bidd him come hither. Commend my hearty love   To Eup.

To Cleopatra . Bidd her feare no ill

From mee at all. What I desire from her

My freedman Thyreus has commission

To utter to her selfe. Epaphroditus,   100

Go see him well rewarded.

Eup.   Health to Caesar   Exeunt
                                                                                Epa. & Eup.

                       Enter Proculeius.

96   hearty] 1639; om. ms
s.d.   Epa. & Eup.] 1639; om. ms

Pro.   The governour is stout, and dooes resolve
To stand th' extreamest hazard of the warre
Before hee yeild Pelusium.
Cæs.   Lett him rue
His stubborne loyalty. Souldiers make ready
For the assault. Tis shame so small a towne
Should stay oure fortunes in the full carreire.   *Exeunt.*

[Act III, Sc. iii]

Antonius *disguis'd like* Timon, *reading.*
Here bury'd doo I ly; thou gentle wave   Callimahi Epigr.
                                                  de Timone.
Keepe hatefull man from treading Timon's grave.
Reader bee gone; enquire no more of mee;
A curse upon thee whatsoere thou bee.
An.   Good, good; ah Timon, Athens nere could boast
A wise philosopher but thee. Thou knew'st
The nature of all men, that all were false.
True Timon true, they are all knaves indeed.
Thou wisely hat'st that wicked thing call'd man,
Whome other fond philosophers admire,   10
And call a noble creature, and partaker
Of divine nature. They were fooles, fooles Timon.
All other sects were fooles, and I will follow
No sect but thine; I am a Timonist.

1 Callinahi...Timone.] 1639; Callimachus ms

That's not enough; Timon himself I am.

    Enter Lucilius, Aristocrates.

Lu. Yonder hee sitts; see Aristocrates
How much unlike the great Antonius,
Whose person late so many legions guarded,
So many kings attended as theire Lord.

Ari. Antonius, where? Thou art deceiv'd Lucilius, 20
That's Timon man.

Lu.   How canst thou jest at this
This wofull passion, which alone's enough
To melt his foes and Cæsar into teares?

Ari. Wee feede this foolish passion, to give way,
And keepe aloofe thus. I'll goe to him. Timon.

An. Ha! What art thou? Bee gone I say from mee.
Gett you to Cæsar man, I hate you all.

Ari. I hate thee Timon. Doost thou thinke tis love
Has brought mee hither? I am come to vexe thee.

An. Oh welcome. What's thy name? Ist Alcibiades? 30

Ari. Hast thou forgott mee?

An.   Doost thou hate all men?

Ari. Why doost thou thinke mee so unnaturall
To love a man? But may wee not love women?

An. Yes, they may bee belov'd, provided alwayes
That they bee false.

Ari.   True Timon, wicked women

May bee belov'd because they ruine men.

An.   Right, right; and now I thinke better upon't
I'll sett no gallowses or gibbetts upp
As I entended once for men to come
And hang themselves. I'll keepe a bawdy house.   40

Ari.   A better way by farre; twill ruine moe.
I wonder Timon at that foolish plott
That I have heard, that in thy gardens once
In Athens thou didst sett upp gallowses
For men in discontent to hang themselves.
How few thinkst thou would bee so madd to doo it?
But to a wench they'll come; and then the office
That thou shalt have will bee of more account.
For where have you a man of any fashion
That now adayes turnes hangman? But a Pandar   50
Is an employment that befitts a statesman,
A thing requires good parts and gravity.

An.   I'd try that course; but tis too slow a plott.
Oh for a speedy way to kill the world!
I have done somewhat in my dayes; my warrs
And bloody battells were not made in vaine.
For I was once Antonius and a Roman,
As in the warrs of Troy Pythagoras
Before that transmigration of his soule
Had beene Euphorbus.

Ari.   Thou art like him still.   60

An.   And when I was Triumvir first at Rome

Ari.   That was a time indeed; then I could heare
Of those good deedes which must bee still a comfort
To youre good consciences though they bee past.
When Rome was fill'd with slaughter, flow'd with blood.
But they perchance were knaves that were proscrib'd,
And might have done more mischeife had they liv'd.

An.   No, they were honest men. I look'd to that.

Ari.   Twas well and carefully.

An.   Behold the list.
But one among the rest most comforts mee,   70
That talking fellow <u>Cicero</u>, that us'd
To taxe the vicious times, and was, forsooth,
A lover of his countrey.

Ari.   Out upon him.
Then hee was rightly serv'd. For is it fitt
In a well govern'd state such men should live
As love theire countrey? Had't not beene for him
Catiline's plott had thriv'd.

An.   Tis true; I'm sure
<u>Caesar</u> was on that side; hee favour'd it.

Ari.   Yes, Cæsar understood himselfe; there's hope
That this young Cæsar too will proove as good   80
A patriot as ere his father was.

An.   Hee will doo reason man; hee is of nature

   Cruell enough. In that proscription
  It did appeare. But now hee'll reigne alone.
Ari. Oh for such factions as were then afoot
  To rend the state, and fill the world with slaughter!
An. Oh lett mee hugge thee <u>Alcibiades</u>.

    <u>Enter</u> Canidius, Lucilius.

<u>Ca</u>. Is that hee yonder? What strange shape is that?
<u>Lu</u>. None talkes with him but <u>Aristocrates</u>,
  Whoo following his owne way, and suiting just   90
  With his conceit, thinkes to reclaime him so.
<u>Ca</u>. The newes that I shall bring will make him worse,
  And fright that little reason, that is left
  Quite from his breast.
<u>Lu</u>.   It cannot soe, <u>Canidius</u>;
  Perchance to heare th' extremity of all
  Will cure his fitt. It cannot make him worse,
  For death it selfe were better and more noble.
<u>Ca</u>. How weake a thing is man that seates his hopes
  In Fortunes slippery and unconstant favours,
  And seekes no surer strengths to guard his soule!   100
  Wanting a strong foundation hee is shaken
  With every winde, orethrowne by every storme.
  And what so frequent as those storms of Fortune?
  Whose fairest weather never brings assurance

84 Speech prefix <u>om</u>.] 1639; appeare. <u>Ari</u>. But ms
85 <u>Ari</u>.] 1639; <u>om</u>. ms
94 <u>Canidius</u>] 1639; my Lord ms

Of perpetuity. But come what will

I'll tell him all.

Lu.   Doo good Canidius.

An.   Well Alcibiades, I am resolv'd

I'll to the warrs againe, and either conquer

Mine enemyes, or take a course to starve

And kill upp my owne souldiers, and so bee   110

Reveng'd on some body. One of these two

May easily bee brought to passe. How think'st thou?

Ari.   Yes yes, but lett's to Court, and there consult.

            Enter Mardio.

See whoo comes here. Now for oure bawdy project.

Heere is a servant I must needs preferre

Well vers'd in bawdry, Master of the art.

Come neer brave Mardio, come.

Mar.   My businesse

Is not to you.

Ari.   Marke him but well, and tell mee

How hee would execute the place.

Mar.   My Lord,

The Queene entreates youre presence at the Pallace   120

The greived Queene, whoo in youre absence pines,

106 Canidius] 1639; my Lord ms
115 I must needs preferre] 1639; fitt for that employment. ms
116 Well...art.] 1639; Master of th' art. Come Mardio.
     Mar. My businesse ms
117 Come....businesse] 1639; Is not to you. Ari. Marke him
     but well, and tell mee ms

                             52

     Whoo suffers in youre greife.

Air.   Well urg'd old Eunuch.

An.   Ha, what of her? Will shee revolt to Caesar?

Mar.   Shee's farre from that my Lord.

An.   What is't hee sayes?

Ari.   Hee sayes the constitution of her body
 Cannot hold out unlesse you visite her.

Mar.   The Queene shall know it, Aristocrates.

Ari.   Did you not say shee pin'd, and languish'd s^r?
 And what's the difference? Tell youre tale youre selfe.

An.   What dooes she say? Dooes shee not hate mee man?   130

Mar.   Oh no, my Lord, shee loves you as her life.
 No spite of fortune that shee has endur'd,
 Or can herafter feare, greives her so much
 As dooes youre absence and strange melancholly.

Ari.   Well Mardio thou art fittest for the place.

Ca.   My lord Antonius.

An.   Ha! Moe men upon us!

Ca.   I come to bring thee heavy newes, Antonius.
 The forces all, which thou didd'st leave encamp'd
 At Actium, horse and foot are gone to Caesar,
 And all th' auxiliary kings. No strength   140
 At all is left thee, but what here thou hast
 At Alexandria.

An.   Ha!

Lu.   This sinkes into him.

Ca.   It makes a deepe impression in his passion.

Ari.   And may perchance expell his other fitt.

An.   All you here yett? Then I have frends I see.
But tell mee, can you bee so mercifull
As to forgive that most unmanly fitt
I have beene it? Oh I am all in blushes.

Ca.   My Lord, take better comfort.

An.   Dearest frends,
I will bee proofe 'gainst any fortune now.   Plutarch.   150
Come, lett's together to the Court, and there
Drowne saddnesse in rich cupps of Meroë wine,
And laugh at Fortunes malice; for youre sight
More cheeres my spirits then her frownes can dull them.
                                                Exeunt.

             Actus Quartus [Sc. i]

             Cleopatra, Glaucus.

Gla.   Madam, all druggs with paine and torment kill,
That kill with speede. No easy way to death
Is wrought but by a slow, and lingring course,
Where Natures strength is by degrees subdu'd,
And yeilding so decayes insensibly.
No art at all can make a drugg that's quicke,
And gentle too. No poison but the Aspe

Of all the mortall brood of Libyaes snakes

Kills with a suddaine and yett easy death,   Plutarch.

As if brought forth to contradict oure skill   10

By envious Nature, whoo disdaines fraile man

Should hope to finde her secretts wholly out.

None but that Serpent, Madam, can effect

What you desire. Of which I here have brought.

Cle.   Leave it good <u>Glaucus</u>; leave the potion too.

Tis quicke thou sayst.

Gla.   Yes Madam; but too painfull

And violent.

Cle.   Well, leave them both with mee.

Lett none adventure on prosperity   <u>Exit</u> <u>Glaucus</u>.

But with a spiritt still prepar'd to dy.

Lett them keepe certaine death still in theire power   20

That dare bee great and happy. Nought but that

Frees states when they are fall'n. Well did wise

And liberall Nature on mankinde bestow

A guift so soveraigne as power to dy.

An Antidote 'gainst Fortunes cruelty.

This is the deare preservative that must

Controll the spite of Fortune, and redeem

A wofull life from loathed servitude.

```
21  Nought but that ] 1639; that alone ms
22  Frees...fall'n. ] 1639; Can cure a ruin'd fortune. ms
27  Controll...redeem ] 1639, om. ms
28  A wofull ] 1639; Redeeme a ms
```

55

    One venome's gentle: tother rough and cruell.
    But tis not safe to trust mine Honour so   30
    On doubtfull propps. The poisons both may faile,
    Or differ farre from what vaine fame reports
    Theire operation. Tis experience
    That must confirme mee. <u>Mardio</u> is return'd.

        <u>Enter</u> Mardio <u>with</u> <u>two</u> <u>prisoners</u>.

<u>Mar</u>.   Here are two men, Madam, condemn'd for murther
    To cruell death, and are to dy tomorrow.
<u>Cle</u>.   Come neerer both, and tell mee, dare you dy?   <u>Dio</u>.
<u>1 pri</u>. Great Queene necessityes strict law imposes
                                              <u>Plutarch</u>.
    That doome upon us. In forc'd actions
    Courage can have no tryall.
<u>Cle</u>.   Dare you dy   40
    A lesse dishonourable way, to scape
    The common hangman's hand, and from a Queene
    Receive youre death, and that an easyer death?
<u>Ambo</u>.   Most willingly great Queene, wee are prepar'd.
<u>Cle</u>.   Give them theire lotts <u>Mardio</u>, the shortest lott
    Is to dy first.
<u>2 pri</u>.   That lott is mine.
<u>Cle</u>.   The Aspe shall bee thy fate. Now Aspe confirme
    What fame reports of thee. Stay thou thy draught

37 <u>Dio</u>.] 1639; <u>om</u>. ms
38 <u>Plutarch</u>.] 1639; <u>om</u>. ms

Till hee bee dead. Feel'st thou no paine?

<u>2 pri</u>. A faintnesse seizes mee, and I would sleepe. 50

<u>Mar</u>.   How gently hee lyes downe, and scarsely strives
Against his death at all.

<u>Cle</u>.   I thinke hee's dead
Already. Sure hee feeles but little paine.
I am confirm'd.

<u>Mar</u>.   Hee's dead and stiffe already.

<u>Cle</u>. Wee'll try no more. As for thy draught of poison
Thus wee discharge thee of it, and from death
Doom'd by the law oure royall pardon frees thee.
Publish it <u>Mardio</u>.

<u>Pri</u>.   All the Godds preserve
Royall and gratious <u>Cleopatraes</u> life.   <u>Exeunt</u>.

<u>Cle</u>. I am resolv'd. Nought but the Libyan Aspe 60
Shall bee renown'd for <u>Cleopatraes</u> death.
Thou pretious worme, that canst redeeme alone
The losse of honour at a rate so easy,
That kill'st as gently as the hand of age,
And art miscall'd a plague of Affrica,
Since thou alone mak'st barren Affrike envy'd
By other lands, though fruitfull, wanting thee;
Whoo crosse the Seas, and thence at highest price
Transport the Aspe as choisest merchandise.
On thee I trust. One gentle touch of thine 70
Can free this life from loathed servitude,

From <u>Cæsar's</u> triumph, the base peoples mocks,
Proud <u>Liviaes</u> scorne, and madd <u>Octaviaes</u> spite.
But why are all my thoughts turn'd to despaire?
Why thinke I now of death? Meethinkes my Genius
Checks this cold feare, and Fortune chiding tells mee
I am ungratefull to distrust her now.
My race of life and glory is not runne,
Nor <u>Cleopatraes</u> Fortunes yett arriv'd
At that great height that must eternize her,   80
And fixe her glorious name above the starrs.
I long to heare what answere <u>Cæsar</u> sends.
I doo not know his temper. But hee's young,
And why should I despaire? Are <u>Cupid's</u> fires
Extinguish'd quite? Are all his arrowes spent?
Or is this beauty, that can boast the conquest
Of <u>Julius Cæsar</u>, and great <u>Antony</u>,
So waned now, it cannot moove the temper
Of one, whome youth makes fitt for Cupid's conquest?

<u>Enter</u> Euphronius, Thyreus.

Eup.   Madam, youre guifts were gratiously receiv'd,   90
And <u>Cæsar</u> with a smiling brow return'd
All seeming love and frendshipp. Hee has sent
His freedman <u>Thyreus</u> to attend youre highnesse,
And to impart his counsells to youre eare.
Cle.   Hee's welcome to us. What's great <u>Cæsar's</u> will?
<u>Exit</u> Eup.

Thy.   Cæsar's best wishes royall Cleopatra
None but youre fairest selfe can ratify.
No power on earth can give what Caesar wants
But you great Queene; for lett youre Majesty
Give creditt to poore Thyreus, though the meanest   100
Of all the servants that attend on Cæsar,
There's none about him is more neere in trust
To whome hee's pleased to impart his thoughts
And secrest wishes. Nothing but youre love
Can crowne his happinesse.

Cle.   Wee are no subject
For Cæsar's mocks though in oure worst of fortune.

Thy.   You are the Queene of fortune, and still hold
A lasting scepter ore that fickle Goddesse
(Fickle to others, to you true and constant).
Youre radiant light lends that blind Goddesse eyes,   110
And guides her to youre service, making all
Actions, nay losses, stepps to greater honour.
The late defeat at Actium, which youre errour
Perchance miscalls a losse, was Fortunes labour
To make you greater, and remoove youre brightnesse
Which was ill plac'd (as Diamonds coursly sett)
From old Antonius to young Cæsar's love
A fitter sphære for those faire eyes to shine in.

Cle.   Without these courtings, Thyreus, if great Caesar

Please to embrace oure frendshipp, wee and Aegypt 120
Shall doo him faithfull service.

<u>Thy</u>. Mighty Queene,
If my rude speech have err'd, I humbly begge
That you would please to thinke it zeale in mee
To doo my master service, and such service
As hee esteemes the best, to gaine youre love.
I oft have heard him (lett youre Majesty
Not bee offended with that truth I utter)
Ravish'd with fame of youre perfections
And noble spiritt, call Antonius happy,
Whome Fortune brought to Aegypt, to behold 130
That Queene whom hee so much desir'd to see.
But when his eyes beheld youre portraiture
Drawne by a skillfull and a faithfull hand,
Hee oft would say it was a likely seat
To hold those Graces. Such perfections
Were fitt for none but <u>Caesar's</u> to admire.

<u>Cle</u>. There was a <u>Caesar</u> lov'd mee once, but I
Am not so proud to thinke it was my meritt.
Though hee would say I did deserve farre more
Then hee could utter, that great <u>Julius</u>, 140
Whose name, and actions fill'd the triple world.

<u>Thy</u>. Though all in him were great, yett nothing greater

131 whom] 1639; that ms
142 nothing greater] 1639; nought more great ms

Then his adopting so divine an heire.

This Cæsar, Madam, for youre dearest love

Besides that power and greatnesse, which the world

Both knows and fears, brings such a youth and beauty

To pleade for him, as in a meane estate

Might moove a Princesse love. Which that youre eyes

May better read, I heere from him present

His true, and most unflatter'd portraiture.   150

Cle.   The fairest forme that ere these eyes beheld.

Where all the best of each best modell meetes.

Cupid's sweete smiles lodg'd in the eye of Mars,

Ganymed's cheeke, th' Imperiall brow of Jove,

Wher love and Majesty are proud to dwell.

Thy.   His age, great Queene, is yett not thirty yeares.

Cle.   I nere till now saw beauty. But Thyreus

May wee repose a confidence in thee

As oure true frend? Wee will deserve thy love.

Thy.   To doo divinest Cleopatra service   160

Is all poore Thyreus pride. In serving you

I best discharge my duty to my master.

Cle.   Then breifely thus; because I would not have

Any take notice of long privacy

Twixt thee and mee, and instantly wee expect

Antonius heere, I will devise some meanes

---

145   power...world] 1639; greatnesse which the world adores ms
146   Both...a] 1639; Brings such a freshnesse both of ms
149   better] 1639; clearely ms
153   .Imperiall] 1639; imperious ms

How to deserve great Caesar's love, and act

What hee shall thanke us for. Meane while stay here

With us, good Thyreus, for wee cannot yett

Dispatch thee with that message wee entend.   170

Thy.   I will attend your highnesse.

Cle.   Till anone

Farewell, good Thyreus; but be near about us.   Exit
                                                      Thyreus.
What more then this could all the fates contrive?

What more then Caesar's love could I have wish'd

On which all power, all state, and gloryes waite?

But oh the weake and fluctuating state

Of human frailty still too much deprest

Or rais'd too much twixt feares and flattring hopes.

Yett hence base feare; a Princely confidence

Fitts Cleopatraes minde and beauty better.   180

        Enter Antonius, Canidius, Lucilius,
              Aristocrates.

My dearest lord!

An.   Ah sweetest Cleopatra,

In this embrace and this Ambrosiake kisse

I am againe possest of all my wealth,

Of all my fortunes. Had the angry Godds

Purpos'd to wreake theire fury fully on mee

They had not left my life so sweete a comfort.

171 attend...anone] 1639; bee ready to attend youre
     highnesse. Exit Thyreus. ms
172 Farewell...s.d.] 1639; om. ms
174 I] 1639; wee ms

Cle.   Possest of you I stand above the reach
Of Fortunes threatning or proud Caesar's power.
Nought but youre greife and melancholly had
Power to deject my spiritts.

An.   Thy true worth   190
Deserves a happier frend, that could bestow
Not take alone his happinesse from thee.
In thy sweete love, and these my faithfull frends
I still am happy; I have lost no frends.
All that are gone from mee to Caesar's side
Ingratefull Titius, and Domitius,
Plancus, Silanus, Dellius, and Hipparchus
Were fortunes frends not mine.

Cle.   Lett's in and feast.
This day wee'll dedicate to mirth and freedome
To crowne youre welcome hither.

An.   Sweetly spoken.   200
Let not a woman teach us souldiers
To be magnanimous.

Cle.   This feast we'll stile
The feast of fellow-dyers.   For no band   Plutarch.
No ty of frendshipp is so firme as that.
They live in love, that meane to dy togither.   Exeunt.

201 Lett...souldiers] 1639; Come worthy frends; lett not a
     woman teach ms
202 To...stile] 1639; Us souldiers courage. Wee will
     stile oure feast ms

[Act IV, Sc. ii]

Caesar, Agrippa, Titius, Plancus, Arius.

Caes.   Grave <u>Arius</u>, in thy troubled lookes I read
Feare for thy native Alexandria.
But banish feare, and know thy power with Caesar.
If they obey oure summons, none shall dy.
But though to th' utmost they resist, thy will
Shall rule oure justice.

Ar.   Humble <u>Arius</u>
Is too much honour'd in great <u>Caesar's</u> favour.

Caes.   Wee give but what wee ow. A debt so great
As mine to thee can nere bee overpay'd.
Great Alexander, whose victorious hand
Founded that city, whose eterniz'd name
For ever honours it, though in great deedes
Hee past oure glory farre, shall not exceede
<u>Caesar</u> in piety. Hee oft would say
Hee ow'd a better beeing to his Master
Then to his father; one meere naturall:
The other mentall, and diviner farre.

        <u>Enter</u> Epaphroditus with Fergusius.
Whoo's that?

Epa.   Fergusius the philosopher,
Condemn'd to death by you.

Cæs.   Dispatch him then.

Epa.   Hee craves a word with Arius ere hee dy.   20

Ar.   What is it brother?

Fer.   Ah good Arius
Wisemen, if truly wise, save wise men still.   Plutarch.

Ar.   Most mighty Cæsar.

Cæs.   Arius no more,
I know what thou desir'st; Fergusius live;
That thou know'st him has sav'd thee.

Fer.   Victory
And fame still wait on Cæsar.

Cæs.   Lett's away,
And march with speede to Alexandria.

Agr.   Cæsar, youre horse are weary. Tis not fitt
Too much to toile them. For I feare a Salley
From Alexandria.

Cæs.   They dare not man.   30

Agr.   Antonius is strong in well provided,
And skillfull horsemen, and despaire of favour
(since twice you have refus'd his propositions)
Will put another valour into him.

Cæs.   What conquest can Antonius hope for heere?

Agr.   His hopes (as neere as I conjecture them)
Are to breake through youre troopes, and gett to sea.

For yett hee has a fleete, that may transport him
To other lands, to gather new supplyes.
But any fortune would proove higher farre   40
To him, then staying heere, without all hope
To bee shutt upp in a beseidged towne.
In my opinion lett youre march bee slow
And gentle, that the horse may bee refresh'd,
And wee prevent the worst.

Cæs.   Lett it bee so.   Exeunt.

[Act IV, Sc. iii]

Lucilius, Aristocrates.

Lu.   How formelesse is the forme of man, the Soule,
How various still, how different from it selfe!
How falsely call'd Queene of this little world!
When shee's a slave, and subject not alone
Unto the bodyes temperature, but all
The stormes of Fortune.

Ari.   What occasion
Makes thee thus offer at Philosophy?

Lu.   Where hast thou liv'd, thou shouldst not know th'
                                                    occasion?
The fitts and changes of Antonius
Are theame enough. How strange a loving soule   10
Is the late hater of mankinde become!

Ari.   That is not strange. Hee's out of breath with
                                              cursing,
And now tis time to stopp his mouth with kissing.

But what can hee conceive of this same Thyreus,

That holds such secrett conference with her?

Lu.   Hee cannot choose but see it.

Ari.   Unless love

Have blinded him; shee carryes it so plainely.

Well, I shall thinke if there bee knavery in't,

(As knavery there must bee) that Cleopatra

Is not so subtle as wee tooke her for.   20

Lu.   Hee must bee told it, if hee will not see.

Upon my life there is some plott of treason

Which yett may bee discover'd.

Ari.   Here they come.

Lett us goe fetch Antonius if wee can.   Exeunt.

    [Act IV, Sc. iv]

    Cleopatra, Thyreus.

Cle.   Pelusium shall bee rendred upp to Caesar   Dio.
                                                        Plutarch.
By oure command to our leiutenant there

Seleucus, those obedience wee not doubt.

Thy.   Noblest of Queenes, you make Imperiall Caesar

As much a debtor to youre curtesy

As hee's already captive to youre beauty.

Cle.   Nor doo wee wrong <u>Antonius</u> at all

In giving upp a towne which is oure owne.

It may bee thought tis done to weaken him.

Alas <u>Antonius</u> is already fall'n   10

So low, that nothing can redeeme him now,

Nor make him able to contest with <u>Caesar</u>.

Hee has not only lost his armyes strength,

But lost the strength of his owne soule, and is not

That <u>Antony</u> hee was when first I knew him.

I can doo <u>Caesar</u> now no greater service,

Though I shall never want a heart to doo it.

But wee shall quickly see th' event of things.

<u>Antonius</u> now is desperate, and putts

His hopes upon the fortune of one Sally;   20

Which will bee suddainly perform'd, before

That thou canst beare a message back to <u>Caesar</u>.

        Antonius, Lucilius, Aristocrates.

An.   Hands on that <u>Thyreus</u> there, to prison with him.

<u>Thy</u>.   To prison?

An.   Yes, away with him I say.

<u>Thy</u>.   <u>Caesar</u> would not have us'd youre messenger

So ill.

An.   Thou art no messenger to mee.

Cle.   For my sake dearest Lord.

An.   Oh for youre sake?
                                              <u>Plutarch</u>.

```
        I cry you mercy Lady.  Beare him hence.      Exit Thyreus.
        I had forgott that Thyreus was youre servant.
        But what strange act should hee performe for you?              30
        Is it to helpe you to a happier frend?
    Cle.    Can you suspect it?  Was my truest Love
        So ill bestow'd?  Can hee, for whose deare sake
        A Queene so highly borne as I preferr'd
        Love before fame, and fondly did neglect
        All names of honour when false Fulvia,              Plutarch.
        And proud  Ocatvia had the name of wives
        Requite mee thus?  Ungratefull Antony,
        For now the fury of a wronged love
        Justly provokes my speech.
    An.                  Oh Cleopatra,                                 40
        It is not Thyreus, but this heart of mine
        That suffers now, deepe wounded with the thought
        Of thy unconstancy.  Did Fortune leave
        One only comfort to my wretched state
        And that a false one?  For what conference
        Couldst thou so oft, and in such privacy
        With Caesar's servant hold, if true to mee?
        Which with the racke I could enforce from him.
        But that I scorne to doo.
    Cle.            You doo not scorne
        To wrong with base unworthy jealousyes                         50
        A faithfull heart.  But if you thinke mee false,
```

Heere sheath youre sword. Make mee the subject rather
Of manly rage then childish jealousy.
It is a nobler crime, and fitter farre
For you to act, easyer for mee to suffer.
For live suspected I nor can nor will.
The lovely Aspe, which I with care have kept,
And was entended a preservative
'Gainst Caesar's cruelty, I now must use
Against Antonius basenesse, a worse foe   60
Then Caesar is. Farewell till death approve
That I was true, and you unjust in love.
An.   Stay Cleopatra, dearest love, forgive mee.
Lett not so small a winde have power to shake
A love so growne as ours. I did not thinke
That thou wert false. My heart gave no consent
To what my tongue so rashly uttered.
Nor could I have outliv'd so sadd a thought.
Lett Thyreus bee releast, and sent to Caesar.

   Enter Canidius.
Ca.   Now is the time to sally forth my Lord,
The foe is tir'd with marching, and youre horse
Are ready all, and waite the signall only.
The least delay looses the action.
An.   I come Canidius. Dearest love farewell.
Few howers will tell thee what Antonius is.   Exeunt.

<u>Cle.</u>   How timorous is guilt? How are my thoughts

Distracted saddly now? On every side

My dangers grow. For should <u>Antonius</u>

Returne in safety home, and know what past

Twixt mee and <u>Thyreus</u>, I have lost his heart,   80

And cannot choose but feare him: if hee dy,

I am not confident of <u>Caesar's</u> love.

Twas but a servants tongue I built upon.

Tis best to make all sure. Within there! <u>Eira</u>?

<u>Ei.</u>   Madam?

<u>Cle.</u>   Are all things ready in the tombe?

<u>Ei.</u>   Yes Madam, <u>Carmio's</u> there and <u>Mardio</u>.

<u>Cle.</u>   Then thither will I goe. If fates contrive

A future state of happinesse for mee,

It is my castle: if my death they doome,

I am possest already of a tombe.   <u>Exeunt</u>.   90

Actus Quintus [Sc. i]

Antonius, Lucilius, Aristocrates.

<u>An.</u>   Defeated are my troopes, my fleete revolted.

The seas and lands are lost, and nothing now

Is left Antonius but a Roman hand,

A sword and heart to dy. You truest servants,

Whose faith and manly constancy upbraides

This wicked age, and shall enstruct the next,

Take from a wretched hand this legacy.

For tune has made my will, and nought but this

Can I bequeath you. Carry it to Caesar.

If hee bee noble, it containes enough   10

To make you happyer then Antonius can.

My glasse of life and empire now is runne,

And from this hand expects a period.

Lu.   My Lord, take fairer hopes.

An.   Fy, Fy, Lucilius,

Loose not thy former meritts in persuading

A man, whome once thou lov'd'st, to such a shame

As to preferre a loath'd captivity

Before a noble death. Thy lookes speake greife.

       Enter Eros.

Say Eros, where's the Queene?

Er.   Shee's dead my Lord.

When those unhappy tidings came to her   Dio.   20
                                              Plutarch.
Of youre defeat, shee straight shutt upp her selfe

Within her tombe and dy'd.

An.   Oh Cleopatra,

Why have I lingred thus that thou a woman

Should'st teach so old a souldier how to dy?

Fortune, I blame not thee, I have enjoy'd

What thou could'st give, and on the envy'd topp

8   nought but this] 1639; nothing else ms

Of thy proud wheele have long unshaken stood.

Whome kings have serv'd, and Rome herselfe obey'd,

Whome all the Zones of Earths diffused globe,

That know inhabitants, have knowne and fear'd.   30

Nor is my fall so much degenerate.   Plutarch.

My strength no armes but Roman armes subdue,

And none but Monarch of the world succeedes.

Glutted with life and Empire now I goe

Free and undaunted to the shades below.

Here, Eros, take this sword. Performe the promise

Which thou hast made, to kill mee whensoere

I should command. Make no reply in words.

Er.   I will bee true or dy. Stand faire. Youre Eros

Will bee youre usher to th' Elisian feilds.   Kills   40
                                                himself.
An.   What hast thou done unfaithfull faithfull Eros?
                                                        Dio. Plutarch.
Too kindely cruell, falsely vertuous?

I'll trust no more, to bee no more directed

By such examples. But wee must bee speedy.

The gates ere this time are sett ope to Cæsar.

Faire Cleopatra I am comming now

To dwell with thee, and ever to behold

Thy heavenly figure, where nor time nor death

Shall make divorse of oure eternall loves.

Thus thus I come to thee. Unfaithfull sword,   [Stabs   50
                                                himself.]
I never knew thee slow in giving death

Till this sadd hower. Some frendly hand lend aide,
And with another wound release my soule.

Enter Mardio

Mar. Where is my lord Antonius? Oh sadd sight?
The Queene enclosed in her tombe desir'd
To take her last leave of you.
An.   Is shee living?
Tis welcome newes. Convey mee quickly frends
Oh quickly thither, that I may expire   Dio. Plutarch.
That breath that's left in Cleopatraes armes.   Exeunt.

[Act V, Sc. ii]

Agrippa, Gallus, Epaphroditus, Proculeius,

Citizens.

Agr. Goe you Epaphroditus, and beseidge
The Pallace, to surprise Antonius:
You Proculeius, and Cornelius Gallus,
Goe presently to Cleopatraes tombe;
Woo her with all youre art and eloquence,
With all assurances of Caesar's love
To leave that place, and yeild her person to him.
Spare no attempts of force or policy
To draw thence. For you the citizens
Of Alexandria, cheere youre fainting hearts,

   I'll mediate in youre behalfe to Cæsar

   To spare the city.

Cit.   Thankes to the most noble

       Enter Cæsar, Arius, Titius, Plancus.

   And good Agrippa.

Agr.   Here hee comes himself.

Caes.   The palenesse of youre feare declares youre guilt.

   But that, though nere so great, shall not exceede

   Oure clemency, to lett you know it was

   Youre happinesse to bee subdu'd by us.

   Mercy shall rule oure just severity.

   First for youre founder Alexander's sake;   Dio.
                                                      Plutarch.
   Next for the love of reverend Arius   20

   Oure Master heere, whose goodnesse farre outweighs

   All of youre offences, and rebellions.

Cit.   Cæsar in goodnesse, as in greatnesse beares

   Aequality with Jove.

         Enter Achoreus.

Acho.   Haile mighty Cæsar.

Caes.   What's hee?

Ar.   Achoreus, Osiris preist,

   A good and holy man.

Caes.   Wee dare beleeve thee,

   And therefore welcome him.

Acho.   Please it great Cæsar
To give Achoreus leave to wait on him
Into the ancient temples of oure Godds
To shew th' Aegyptian rites and mysteryes,   30
And all the Deityes that wee adore?

Cæs.   Most willingly Achoreus I would see
Godds, but not oxen.

Ti.   Hee has blank'd the Preist.   Dio.
                                                    Sueton.
Cæs.   I faine would see great Alexander's hearse
The mansion once of so divine a Soule
A spirit greater then the world it selfe,
Whome the world fear'd, but could not satisfy.

Acho.   Within the vault of oure Pyramides
His body yett all whole may Cæsar see,
And all the bodyes of oure Ptolomeys.   40

Cæs.   I'd see kings only, not dead carcasses.   Dio.
                                                    Sueton.
But see, Epaphroditus is return'd.

        Enter Epaphroditus, Lucilius, Aristocrates.

Cæs.   Speake man, where is Antonius?

Epa.   Slaine, my Lord.

Cæs.   How slaine? What hand durst doo it?

Epa.   His owne hand.

Cæs.   That was oure feare. Cruell Antonius,
Too cruell to thy self, to Rome and mee.

How white a day have all the people lost?
How great might Caesar's happinesse have beene
Had but the fates permitted mee to lay
These conquering arms aside, and once againe   50
Embrace thee, deare Antonius, as a frend!
Thou worthy aider of my Infant fortunes,   Plutarch.
Thou brave revenger of great Julius death,
Witnesse these teares though I were forc'd to warre
(Whilest thou preferring forreine love before
Caesar's alliance, did'st reject my kindred,
And scorne my love) I still could honour thee.
But since too cruell fate denyes to mee
So great an happinesse, as to expresse
This love to thee alive, lett thy deare ghost   60
Behold my Piety, and see the honours
Caesar will doo to thy sadd funerall.

Lu.   Most royall Caesar-like dissimulation.   [Aside.]
Ari.   I hope how ere, twill serve oure turnes Lucilius.
Now is the fittest time.
Caes.   What men are these?
Eba.   Two of Antonius truest servants, Caesar,
Whoo bring a letter from theire dying Lord.
Caes.   Lett me peruse it. Well, it shall bee granted.
Youre lives and fortunes both are safe, and since
Wee ever lov'd fidelity, you shall   70

52 Plutarch.] 1639; om. ms
54 though I were] 1639; that I though ms
56 my] 1639; his ms
57 my...I] 1639; his frendshipp) ms

If so you like bee welcome to oure service.

Lu.   Tis oure desire; oure lives and fortunes ever

Shall doo great Caesar true and faithfull service

As they before did to Antonius.

Caes.   Where did hee dy?

Epa.   In Cleopatraes armes

By her with ropes lett upp into the tombe

After his deadly wound.

Caes.   Is shee there still?

     Enter Gallus.

Now I shall know. Speake Gallus, what's the newes?

Gall.   Wee came and call'd at Cleopatraes tombe,   Dio.
                         Plutarch.
Whoo from above made answere, and deny'd   80

To yeild herselfe but upon Caesar's word.

I then with best persuasions strove to winne her,

And held her talke a while, whilest Proculeius

On tother side the tombe espy'd a place

That open stood, by which the Queene receiv'd

Dying Antonius, which hee scaling enter'd

Behinde the Queene. But had hee not beene speedy

Shee there had slaine her selfe. A maide of hers

Spy'd Proculeius entring, and aloud

Cry'd out oh Queene thou art surpris'd alive.   90

Shee drawing a short ponyard was restrain'd

By <u>Proculeius</u>, whoo both held her hands,
And spake her faire; at last obtain'd so much
By strong persuasions of youre clemency
Hee drew her thence, and gott her to the Pallace;
Where now shee is, and <u>Proculeius</u> stayes.
But her desire is still to speake with you;
Till when from us shee will admitt no comfort.
<u>Cæs</u>.   Wee will in person presently goe see her.
Protect mee <u>Pallas</u> 'gainst false <u>Venus</u> charmes. <u>Exeunt</u> <u>omnes</u>.

[Act V, Sc. iii]

Cleopatra <u>in</u> <u>mourning</u>.

<u>Cle</u>.   Knowne mischeifes have theire cure; but doubts have none,
And better is despaire then fruitlesse hope
Mixt with a killing feare. My thoughts are now
More blacke and balefull then this sadd attire.
If <u>Cæ</u>sar come, I doo not feare his chiding.
I have a certaine Antidote 'gainst that.
Tis not his anger, but his love afflicts
My doubting soule, whither that love will proove
Feigned or true. Yett that may straight appeare;
Hee's not so old, nor I so ignorant   10
But that his actions, gestures, words, and lookes

Will make his heart ly open by my veiw.

            <u>Enter</u> Cæsar, Epaphroditus <u>attending</u>.

<u>Cæs</u>.   How sweete a sorrow dwells upon that brow! [<u>Aside</u>.]
How would shee show in smiling dalliance!
Oh pardon mee thou powerfull Godd of love
That durst presume to tempt thy Deity.
Forgive my confidence; I now excuse
<u>Antonius</u> weakenesse. But stay there my heart.
My vertuous <u>Livia</u> is more faire then shee.

<u>Cle</u>.   Haile mighty Prince; for that high name the   <u>Dio</u>.   20
                                              Godds   <u>Plutarch</u>.
Whoo reft mee of it, have bestow'd on thee.

<u>Cæs</u>.   Rise <u>Cleopatra</u>, <u>Cæsar's</u> victory
Takes nought from you.

<u>Cle</u>.   Oh, lett mee never rise
Till <u>Cæsar</u> grant my suit.

<u>Cæs</u>.   Good Queene stand upp
And freely speake what you desire.

<u>Cle</u>.   I begge
A boone but small, which <u>Cæsar</u> nere deny'd
His greatest enemyes.

<u>Cæs</u>.   And can you thinke
I should deny it you? Doo but expresse it.

<u>Cle</u>.   That thou would'st kill mee <u>Cæsar</u>; I have liv'd
These many yeares too long. I should have dy'd   <u>Dio</u>.   30
When that great Worthy, that renowned <u>Cæsar</u>

Was basely murther'd in Romes Capitoll.

Surviving him was my unhappinesse.

But I have liv'd to see his Sonne inherit

His state and Empire, and controll the world.   Dio.

Cæs.   Bee cheery Cleopatra, feare no wrong

At Cæsar's hands.

Cle.   Death is no wrong at all.

I have deserv'd it s^r.

Cæs.   But can you thinke

That wee, shose clemency so many men

And stubborne enemyes so oft have proov'd,   40

Should now at last bee cruell to a Queene?

But wee must chide you that so long togither

Have sided with Antonius, and with him

Conspir'd the wracke of Rome.   Dio. Plutarch.

Cle.   That's soone excus'd.

If twere a crime to love great Antony

(Which I confesse I did, and his large favours

Truly deserv'd it) thinke it was not mine,

But fates owne crime, that first allotted mee

To his protection. Had youre share of rule

In Aegypt lyen, I had beene Cæsar's frend.   50

Cæs.   Besides with men and money you gave aide

To Caius Cassius in Philippi feild,

Whoo murdred Cæsar in the Capitoll.

Cle.   Cæsar, as false as truth it selfe is true.

I was accused to Antonius					Appianus. Plutarch.

For that before. But in Cilicia

I quickly clear'd those causelesse jealousyes.

Wittnesse thou glorious starre which the great soule

Of noble Julius, when hee left the earth,

Added to heaven, how innocent I am							60

From any fault in that. But Caesar know

Against thy father not the act alone,					Dio.

But even suspition shall bee purg'd with death.

I will no longer live.

Caes.		What have I done?				[Aside.]

I feare my rashnesse has too farre betray'd			Dio.

My thoughts to Cleopatra. Gentle Queene

Bee comforted. Expect at Caesar's hands

Nothing but love and frendshipp. Doo not wrong

My goodnesse with unjust suspition.

All former greivances are quite forgott.					70

Youre houshold servants shall not bee diminished.

Epaphroditus, see the Queene attended

As fits her state and honour; and till next

Wee visite you, rest with a full assurance

Of oure best love and friendship.

Cle.			All the payment

That my poore fortunes can return to you

65 Dio.] 1639; om. ms
71 houshold...diminished.] 1639; port and state shall bee
    maintain'd at full. ms
73 fits...and] 1639; best befitts her royalty. ms
75 best...friendship.] 1639; entirest love. ms

Is thankes and service.

Cæs.   Epaphroditus.

Epa.   Cæsar.   They whisper.

Cle.   Yes, whisper on; you cannot overreach   [Aside.]
My jealousyes. No signes of love at all,
No smile, nor amorous glance; I was deceiv'd,   80
And meerely coosen'd by base Thyreus.   Exit Cæsar.
But I must hide my feares, and cleare this brow
The better to effect my purposes.

Epa.   How fares youre Majesty?

Cle.   Never so well--
As now I am. I did not thinke great Cæsar
Had beene so full of love and curtesy.

Epa.   Oh Madam, Cæsar's th' unexampled mirrour
Of royalty; and dooes as farre exceede
All petty kings in goodnesse as in power.
And if my humblest services in ought   90
May give content to royall Cleopatra,
I shall bee proud to bee commanded still.

Cle.   Thankes good Epaphroditus.
That love is true that's show'd in misery.
But what have I forgott? I had a note
Of some particulars I meant to give
To Cæsar's hand, and quite forgott it heere.
Nor would I trust the carriage of a thing
Of so great consequence to every hand.

Epa.   Will you command my service?

Cle.   I shall rest   100
Indebted to youre love. Cæsar will thanke you,   Dio.
It much concernes both his estate and mine.
Bee speedy good Epaphroditus, for
I long to heare his answere.

Epa.   Feare not, Madam,
A quicke performance. It rejoices mee   [Aside.]
To see her looke so cheerily again.   Exit Epa.

Cle.   So now my trouble is remoov'd, I come,
I come my dearest lord Antonius,
Never till now thy true and faithfull love.
My much abused Lord, doo not disdaine   110
Or blush t' acknowledge Cleopatraes name
When teares, and blood have wash'd her spotted soule.
Wert thou alive againe, not all the world
Should shake my constancy, or make divorce
Twixt thee and mee. But since too late, alas,
My teares of sorrow come, I'll follow thee,
And begge thy pardon in the other world.
All crimes are there for evermore forgott.
There Ariadne pardons Theseus falsehood,
Dido forgives the perjur'd Prince of Troy,   120
And Troilus repentant Cressida.
Though false to thee alive, I now am come
A faithfull lover of thy dust and tombe.   Exit.

[Act V, Sc. iv]

    Agrippa, Gallus, with two Psylls.

Gall.   Marcus Agrippa, I have here provided
As Cæsar gave in charge, two Libyan Psylls.
All Affrike yeilds not fitter for his purpose.

Agr.   They looke like likely ones.

Gall.   They have been proov'd,
And have already on my souldiers,
When they were bitt by serpents, done strange cures
Past all beleefe or hope, recall'd fledd life
Backe to his mansion, and beyond the power
Of Aesculapius have suck'd, and charm'd
The mortall venome from theire dying limms. Plinius, 10
                Solinus, Lucanus.
These two, Agrippa, in theire infancy
Theire doubting sires to try theire lawfull births
(As Eagles try theire Eaglets 'gainst the Sunne)
Expos'd to mortall serpents, and were so
Confirm'd in what they sought. The trembling snakes
Durst not assault the infants.

     Enter Cæsar

Agr.   Heere hee comes.

Cæs.   Are these the men?

Gall.   Yes Cæsar.

Cæs.   Carry them
  To Cleopatraes Pallace. Lett them wait
  Neere to Epaphroditus.

                   Enter Epaphroditus.
                             What's the newes?
  How fares the Queene?

Epa.   Never more cheery s^r.
  Her lookes expresse her hopes, nor in her words
  Can shee conceale her inward cheerefullnesse.
  But one thing, s^r, shee saide shee had forgott,
  Which neerly did concerne both you and her,
  And that in such a cause shee durst not trust
  A common messenger, requesting mee
  To give it to youre hands.

Cæs.   Shee has deceiv'd thee,
  And all of us; the worst that I could feare
  Is come to passe. Oh runne Epaphroditus.
  I'll follow thee with all the speede I can.
  But all too late I feare oure speede will come.   Exeunt.

            [Act V, Sc. V]
     Cleopatra crowned, attended by Glaucus,

19 s.d. at 1. 20 ms

                    Mardio, Eira, Charmio. Shee takes her
                    state. Antony's herse is brought in.

Cle.   This is my second coronation day,
But nobler then the first, and fuller farre
Of reall honour and magnificence.
Nor till this pompous hower was Cleopatra
A perfect Queene. Alas, I did not sway
A scepter over Fortune, or command
As now I doo, the Destinyes themselves.
I wore a painted honour, a meere shadow
Of Regall state, and such a feeble crowne
As warre could threaten, treason undermine,   10
And every puffe of Fortune blow if off.
My state is constant now, my thoughts above
The feare of dangers, or opposing foes.

Mar.   What new addition has shee gott of state?   [Aside.]
Gla.   I cannot tell. Nor can I guesse her meaning.
Cle.   Glaucus and Mardio, leave the roome a while.   Exeunt.
Come hither Girles. I will no longer hide
My joyes from you. In such attire as this
I goe to meete my deare Antonius.

Ch.   Madam, hee's dead.
Cle.   Alas, thou art deceiv'd.   20
Hee lives, my Charmio, in the other world,
And stayes for mee. I have been too too slacke

In comming to him. This that here lyes dead
Was but the house that lodg'd my dearest Lord
That earthly mansion that did once containe
The kindest, noblest, and the truest soule
That ever liv'd. And this oure second meeting
Is farre more sweete, and full of noble love
Then when wee first mett in Cilicia,
When oure magnificence and pompe did fill   30
The world with wonder and astonishment.
Why weepe you Girles? Is it to see youre mistres
Greater then ere in Glory? If you lov'd mee,
You'd weepe to see great Cleopatra ledd
A wretched captive through the streetes of Rome
Before proud Caesar's charriot, mock'd and flouted,
And from a Queene become Octaviaes drudge.
No, no my Girles, I will bee still my selfe,
And from this seat of state looke downe in scorne
On Rome, and Caesar's threats as things below mee.   40
Ei.   Nor here shall my attendance leave you, Madam.
I'll waite upon you to th' Elisian shades.
Ch.   Nor will poore Charmio bee left behinde.
Cle.   My earthly race is runne, and I descend
As great a ghost as Theban Semele,
When her ambitious love had sought and mett
The Thunderers embraces, when no pyle
Of Earthly wood, but Jove's cælestiall fire

Consum'd her beautyes relliques, and sent downe
Her soule from that Majestike funerall. 50
Farewell thou fading remnant of my love.
When I am gone, I'll leave these earthly parts
To keepe thee company, never to part,
But dwell togither, and dissolve togither.
Come Aspe, possesse thy mansion, freely feede
On these two hills, upon whose snowy topps
The winged <u>Cupid</u> oft has taken stand,
And shott from thence the proudest hearts on earth.
Corruption now and rottennesse must seize
This once admired fabricke, and dissolve 60
This flesh to common elements againe.
When skillfull Nature, were shee strictly bound
To search through all her storehouse, would bee pos'd
To tell which peice was <u>Cleopatra</u> once.
Sweete Aspe, I feele thy touch, and life beginns
From these cold limmes to take her gentle flight.
A slumber seizes mee. Farewell my Girles.
Thus lett the Romans finde mee dead, and now
Maugre the power of Rome, and <u>Cæsar's</u> spleene
That <u>Cleopatra</u> liv'd and dy'd a Queene. 70
<u>Ch</u>.   Shee's dead, and <u>Eira</u> too. I heare a noise,
There is no dallying now; I must bee speedy,

52 these...parts] 1639; this earth of mine ms

And use the common, and sure way to death.   *Stabbs herselfe.*

   Enter Cæsar, Agrippa, Titius,

    Plancus, Gallus, Epaphroditus,

     Proculeius, Thyreus.

Cæs. Wee come too late, and all in vaine I feare
Oure care has beene.

Epa. Here lyes her servant bleeding,
Not dead; speake Charmio, how dy'd the Queene?

Ch. A death that well beseem'd her royall birth. *Dyes.*

Agr. See Cæsar see; the marke upon her breast,
And here the fatall authour.

Cæs.   'Twas the Aspe.
Bee speedy now, and use youre utmost power Sueton. 80
                 Dio.
You skillfull Psylls; call backe this royall soule
To her faire seat, and take from Cæsar's bounty
Above youre wish. Sucke thou the wounded place,
And mutter thou thy strongest charms to fright
Pale death from thence. And you infernall Godds,
If ere to human prayers you could lend
An exorable eare, tis Cæsar beggs,
Cæsar, whose sword has sent to youre blacke shades
An hundred thousand soules, and still has power
T'enlarge youre Empire, begs in lieu of all   90

77 beseem'd] 1639; became ms
90 begs] 1639; craves ms

But restitution of one soule alone.

Ti.　　　　　How royally shee dy'd!

Pla.　　　　　　　　　　No conquer'd Prince
Did ever finde a nobler way to death.
Had feeble Perseus knowne so brave a course,
Hee had redeem'd his captive life from shame,
And not depriv'd the conquerour of fame.

Cæs.　　　　Is there no hope?

Psy.　　　　　　　　　　Shee's gone past all recovery.

Cæs.　　　　Wee will no longer strive 'gainst Destiny.
Though thou art dead, yett live renown'd for ever,
And lett this action speake thee to the world　　　　　　　　100
A foe not shaming Cæsar's victory.
No other crowne, or scepter after thine
Shall Aegypt honour. Thou shalt bee the last
Of all the reigning race of Ptolomey.
And all, and more then what thy letter crav'd
Will Cæsar grant. With dead Antonius
In richer state then ere proud Memphis saw
Her kings enterr'd, shall Cleopatra ly.　　　　Sueton. Dio.
　　　　　　　　　　　　　　　　　　　　　　　Plutarch.
Thy dying figure carv'd in fairest stone
Shall my triumphant charriot weare, for all　　　　　　　　110
To gaze and wonder at thy forme and worth.
Aegypt no more a kingdome, now a Province

92　dy'd?] 1639; sitts! ms; dy'd!] dy'd? 1639
109　fairest] 1639; richest ms

<u>Cornelius</u> <u>Gallus</u>, is thy government.

And here lett <u>Cæsar</u> sheath the civil sword;

Whose fatall edge these twenty yeares has ript

The bleeding entrails of afflicted Rome.

Heere lett oure labours end. Advance, brave frends,

Oure prosperous Eagles home to Italy,

To reape the fruit of all oure warrs and toiles,

And fill great Rome with conquer'd Aegypts spoiles.   120

Finis.

Appendix 1.

A list of accidentals altered from the copy-text.
Silent alterations are not included.

I i

36   strength] 1639; strenght ms
38   Majesty] 1639; Mai^{e}sty ms
53   Side note. Plutarch] ; Plutarh ms

I ii

s.d. Euphronius] 1639; Euphroneus ms
59   blest.] 1639; ∼$_\wedge$ ms
174 means,] 1639; ∼. ms
208 Through] 1639; Throug ms
231 Consuls] ∼$_\wedge$ ms; ∼, 1639

II i

28   give.] 1639; ∼, ms
99   countrey.] 1639; ∼$_\wedge$ ms

II iii

86   matchlesse] 1639; matclesse ms
101 counsells?]∼?, ms; ∼, 1639
104 And∼I,] 1639; ∼, ∼$_\wedge$ ms

119 power,] ∼. ms, 1639

II iv

48 lightning] 1639; ligthning
93 owne,] ∼‸ ms; ∼‸1639
112 endure.] 1639; ∼‸ms

III ii

80 hither] 1639; higher ms (with a "t" written over the "g")

III iii

41 moe.] ∼‸ms; ∼, 1639
57 For] 1639; (For ms
96 worse,] ∼. ms, 1639
99 favours,] 1639; ∼, ms
121 pines,] 1639; ∼. ms
124 Lord.] 1639; ∼: ms
143 passion.] 1639; ∼; ms

IV i

109 constant).] ∼)‸ ms, 1639
198 mine.] 1639; ∼‸ms

IV iii

54 nobler] 1639; noler ms

V ii

89   and₀ aloud] 1639; ~. ~ms

V iv

11   two,] 1639; ~; ms
19   news?] 1639; ~₀ms
26   requesting] 1639; requsting ms

Appendix 2.

Press-variants in the 1639 edition. Copies collated:
BM (British Museum), Fo (Folger Shakespeare Library),
Yale (Yale University), Hunt (Henry E. Huntington Library),
Harv (Harvard University).

Sheet B (outer forme)

	Corrected	Uncorrected	Undetermined
Sig. B 5.			
I ii 85	not] BM	nor] Fo	Yale, Hunt, Harv
Sig. B 6v.			
I ii 164	supported] Fo, Hunt, Harv	supporred] Yale, BM	
Sig. B 8v.			
II i 17	dignity$_\wedge$] Yale, Fo, Hunt, Harv	~.] BM	
Sig. B 12v.			
II iii 93	behinde] Fo, Hunt, Harv	beh nde] Yale, BM	

Sheet B (inner forme)

Sig. B 10.			
II i 117	time] Fo, Hunt, Harv	tim] Yale	BM

Sheet D (outer forme)

Sig. D.

   IV i 119   these] Yale,   thes] Fo
                  BM, Hunt, Harv

Sig. D. 11.

   V iii 52   Cassius] Fo   C ssi u]   BM, Hunt,
                                     Yale   Harv

Sheet D (inner forme)

Sig. D 5v.

   IV iv 43   unconstancre]   unconstancue]
                  Yale, BM, Harv   Fo
                                         unconstcre]
                                         Junt

Sheet E (inner forme)

Sig. E 2.

   V v 30   fill] Yale,   fil] BM
                Fo, Hunt, Harv

Appendix 3.

Collation of the manuscript and the 1639 edition. Lemmata are those of the present text, and show the manuscript or 1639 form chosen. Variants appear after the bracket. Only substantive and semi-substantive variants are listed.

I i

1   name!] ~∧ 1639
3   pride!] ~? 1639
9   occasion∧] ~ , 1639
11 'tis] ∧~ 1639
14 suffred] suffer'd 1639
15 But,] ~∧1639; Lords,] frends ∧ms
17 pleasures] pleasure 1639
19 spite∧] ~. 1639
20 Tis...true,] tis like enough. ms
21 budd,] ~∧ 1639
24 adulterismes] adulterisme 1639
25 state,] ~∧1639
26 distrest,] ~∧1639
27 brothers] brother's 1639; Court] house ms
30 warre∧] ~ , 1639

33   lover;] ~: 1639
37   beauty,] ~ₐ 1639
38   surely:] ~. 1639
41   powerₐ] ~, 1639
45   fall'n] falne 1639
47   Ti....must] Pl....shall 1639
49   itₐ] ~, 1639
53   Plutarch. in Anton.] Plutarch 1639, at 1. 54
54   familyₐ] ~, 1639
55   ruines] ~ₐruine 1639
57   and,] ~ₐ1639
60   swordsₐ] ~, 1639
61   upp,] ~ₐ 1639
66   seem'd] teem'd 1639
67   this] that ms
71   kingdome] Kingdomes 1639
73   elegance!] ~? 1639
78   them answers,] their~; 1639
87   witts...mee.] wit...~; 1639
89   envyₐ] ~, 1639
97   faultsₐ] ~, 1639
102 oure] or 1639
103 whither] whether 1639
105 usₐ] ~, 1639

107 great,] ~, 1639

108 of;] ~. 1639

110 body.] ~ ? ms

117 Antonius,] ~; 1639

119 freeer,...Cæsar's.] here, ...Cæsars. 1639

120 do] should ms; them,] ~∧1639

123 still obey] ever serve ms; Lords∧] ~, 1639

128 Here...Lords,] om. ms

129 The Queen by mee] My Lords, the Queene ms

131 Mardio,...services∧] Marcio∧...~, 1639

132 friends,] Masters∧ ms

133 austerity∧] ~ , 1639

134 censures∧] ~, 1639

135 try] see ms

I ii

s.d. A feast preparing.] om. ms

1 Glaucus∧] ~, 1639

3 ∧Twould...now;] 'Twould...~, 1639

4 Charmio∧] ~, 1639

5 These] Those 1639

7 admir'd,] ~; 1639
9 lights∧] ~. 1639
13 But art thou sure] But hearke they come. ms

14-15 om. ms

15-16 s.d. A flourish.] om. 1639

18   so; for what]   so, what   1639
21   My Lord,] om. 1639
24   orders_∧] ~, 1639
34   shew!]   show?   1639
37   wexes]   vexes   1639
41   Italy_∧] ~, 1639
43   acceptance.] ~ : 1639
45   _∧Tis] '~1639
48   was_∧] ~, 1639
53   prankes] feats   1639
57   a wit so dull]   so dull a braine ms
58   hee_∧] ~, 1639
59   enjoy_∧] ~, 1639; blest.]~_∧ ms
61   motion_∧] ~, 1639
66   Then_∧   Princes_∧...care]~,~,...~; 1639
70   Munatius] Minutius   1639
73   soule_∧] ~, 1639
74   love_∧] ~, 1639
79   The] This   1639
80   Cleopatra_∧] ~, 1639
81   hold'st_∧]~, 1639
83   Cleopatra,] ~_∧ 1639
84   Cœlosyria_∧] ~, 1639
85   not] ~ , 1639
86   modesty.] ~ : 1639
89   no.] ~ ; 1639

91   aimes.] ~! 1639
93   Unworthinesse₍ₐ₎] ~, 1639
95   not₍ₐ₎] ~, 1639
97   owne,] ~₍ₐ₎ 1639
100 is.] ~; 1639
109 place,] ~₍ₐ₎1639
111 know,] ~₍ₐ₎1639
113 ₍ₐ₎Twas] '~1639
114 wine!] ~. 1639
115 Canidius,] ~; 1639
119 is!] ~, 1639
120 know;] ~, 1639
127 growne!] ~. 1639
128 Munatius₍ₐ₎] Minutius, 1639
143 mee₍ₐ₎] ~, 1639
144 shape₍ₐ₎...strength,] ~,...~₍ₐ₎1639
148 yeild,] ~; 1639
149 captivity₍ₐ₎] ~, 1639
151 now₍ₐ₎] ~, 1639
159 Ti. ₍ₐ₎Twere]om. '~ 1639
160 bee.] ~₍ₐ₎ 1639
162 Ti.] om. 1639
166 Cœlosyria₍ₐ₎] ~, 1639
169 bedd?] ~. 1639
171 Cato₍ₐ₎] ~, 1639

172 Ti....Pla.] om....Ti. ms
173 Plancus] Marcus 1639
174 Ti....,] Pla..... ms
176 vices.] ~; 1639
180 plac'd~] ~, 1639
181 Pla.] Ti. ms
182 Ti.] Pla. ms
183 Plancus] Titius ms
189 king~] ~, 1639
191 acts~] ~, 1639
199 Pla.] Ti. ms
201 sealing~] ~, 1639
205 Speech prefix om.] Pla. ms; ~twixt] '~1639
208 France,...Germany;] ~~ ... ~~ 1639
211 mee~] ~, 1639
213 True,...hope~] ~~ ... ~, 1639
217 th' effeminate] the vicious ms
223 if mad] whither ms
226 so;] ~, 1639
227 her;] ~, 1639
228 Munatius Plancus~] Minutius ~, 1639
229 thoughts.]~~1639
231 Fort....Consuls~] Fort...~, 1639
232 both~ ...Domitius~] ~,...~, 1639
234 Pelusium,] ~, 1639

235 thee.] ∼; 1639

236 businesse₍ₐ₎] ∼, 1639

II i

s.d. <u>Ventidius</u>.] <u>om</u>. ms

2   power,] right: ms

5   heere....are.] ∼;...∼, 1639

6   Axes₍ₐ₎...borne;] ∼,..., 1639

8   assisting.] ∼, 1639

11 was₍ₐ₎] ∼, 1639

12 Fathers₍ₐ₎...face₍ₐ₎] ∼,..., 1639

13 assembly;] ∼, 1639 (pointing questionable in ms)

15 Happy₍ₐ₎] ∼, 1639; for] to ms

17 Consul's] Consuls 1639

19 cause, <u>Antonius</u>,] ∼₍ₐ₎ ∼₍ₐ₎ 1639

20 <u>Cæsar's</u>] Cæsars 1639

24 banishment,...restor'd₍ₐ₎] ∼₍ₐ₎...∼, 1639

27 banishment,...restor'd   ... , 1639

27 price] prize 1639

28 give.] ∼, ms

31 Are tane away;] Remooved else ms

32 thee.] ∼; 1639

33 him.] ∼, 1639

37 which] that 1639

39 Gainst...mean it] '∼...meant 1639

40 dare, <u>Antonius</u>₍ₐ₎] ∼₍ₐ₎∼, 1639

42	Fall'n from obedience]	Revolted from thee 1639
45	action.]	~ : 1639
46	needy.]	~ ; 1639
47	want]	warre ms
49	not:]	~ ; 1639
52	Romans,]	~ ; 1639
54	of...tane,]	om....~: 1639
56	Know,...frends,]	~$_\wedge$ ... ~$_\wedge$ 1639
57	in....thus.]	~; ...~: 1639
64	shipps,]	~$_\wedge$ 1639
65	man'd;]	~ : 1639
68	strength$_\wedge$]	~, 1639
70	warre$_\wedge$]	~, 1639
72	Provinces$_\wedge$ ...all$_\wedge$]	~,...~; 1639
75	That]	The 1639
77	self.]	~: 1639
78	Dio. Plutarch]	om. 1639
81	So....sufferance;]	Ti....~: 1639
82	defensive$_\wedge$]	~, 1639
90	ended$_\wedge$]	~ , 1639
96	so.]	~ , 1639
100-101	s.d. Titius,]	~$_\wedge$ ms
101	list,...mee$_\wedge$]	~;...~; 1639
108	consider'd$_\wedge$ ...frend,]	~,...$_\wedge$ 1639
109	resolved, Marcus,]	~$_\wedge$~. 1639

111 guests] frends ms
112 City favours] Senate favour ms
114 base.] ~ : 1639
116 fury;] ~ , 1639
117 away,] ~ ; 1639

II ii

3   <u>Seleucus</u>,] ~_∧ 1639
5   long.] ~ ; 1639
6   world_∧] ~ , 1639
11 frends_∧...other.] ~ , .. ~: 1639
19 rumour.] ~ ; 1639
20 true....nakedly,] ~ , ...~_∧ 1639

II iii

1   enstruct] entrust 1639
2   moe circumstances,] more ~: 1639
4   <u>Cleopatra</u>,] ~ . 1639
7   prevaile;] ~_∧ 1639
11   suit;] ~ , 1639
15   frend,] ~ ; 1639
18   oppose_∧...know,] ~ ,...~ ; 1639
19   hopes_∧] ~ , 1639
25   her...friends] them frends, that end to mee were fatall. ms
26   Wher's...comes.] <u>om</u>. ms
26-27 s.d. <u>Enter</u> Antonius] Antonius, Cleopatra 1639
30   home_∧] ~ , 1639

31	thou,...know,...so.] ~ˬ...~ˬ...~;	1639
37	wereˬ] ~,	1639
39	company,] ~ˬ	1639
41	dreames;] ~.	1639
42	yours;] ~.	1639
43	beeˬ] ~,	1639
45	feare,] ~:	1639
47	farre.] ~:	1639
49	presenceˬ] ~,	1639
51	else?...thinkeˬ]~;...~,	1639
52	disconsolate.] ~,	1639
53	company;] ~,	1639
54	now.] ~,	1639
55	already,] ~.	1639
60	behinde,] ~ !	1639
64	alas,...mee?] ~!...~,	1639
68	Roman Antony] honourable Roman	ms
69	noble love,] nobler ~;	1639
70-71	Not...houres,] Not as the mistresse of his looser thoughts,	ms
75	Without...other.] om.	ms
77	worth] thoughts	ms
80	Court:] ~;	1639
81	callsˬ] ~,	1639
84	come;]~, 1639; agree] consent	ms
85	frends,] ~ˬ	1639

87   thinke;] ~ , 1639

91   thinke, my Lord, tis fitt] think tis fit, my Lord, 1639

92   warre₍ₐ₎] ~, 1639

93   behinde. Besides,] ~ , ~₍ₐ₎ 1639

95   whome] which 1639; Plutarch] om. ms

97   mee....Kings,] ~ ,... ~₍ₐ₎ 1639

100 whoo] which 1639

101 counsells?] ~ , 1639

104 And₍ₐ₎ I,] ~ ,~₍ₐ₎ ms

106 Titius₍ₐ₎] ~ , 1639

107 helpe,] ~₍ₐ₎ 1639

110 charge,] ~₍ₐ₎ 1639

111 sea.] ~; 1639

112 them;] ~, 1639

120 starrs,] ~₍ₐ₎ 1639

II iv

1   Godds₍ₐ₎] ~? 1639

4   births₍ₐ₎] ~, 1639

5   wombe;] ~. 1639

8   Godds₍ₐ₎] ~, 1639

11   dire] sad 1639

12   bee;] ~, 1639

13   misery:] ~; 1639

15   shutt₍ₐ₎ ...fates₍ₐ₎ ...bookes .] ~,... ~,... ~! 1639

20   upwards] upward 1639

27 has] had 1639
29 prodigyes .] ~ : 1639
34 away;] ~ , 1639
41 Dio.] om. ms
44 feilds,] ~ₐ 1639
45 Speech prefix om.] Se. 1639
52 standₐ] ~ , 1639
53 conquerour.] ~ , 1639
55 fought....all;] ~ : ... ~ , 1639
58 gott,] ~ₐ 1639
59 conquests] conquest 1639
61 powerₐ] ~ , 1639
70 enoughₐ] ~ , 1639
74 I'll go within,] I will goe in ms
75 Se.] Gla. 1639
77 Gla.] Se. 1639
80 Mar....strangest] Speech prefix om....strongest 1639
83 it.] ~ : 1639
85 beforeₐ] ~ , 1639
89 drumms,] ~ . 1639
90 'gainst] against 1639
91 Dio.] om. ms
93 rest.] ~ : 1639
95 towne,...foesₐ] ~ₐ... ~ , 1639

97 vanquished.] ~, 1639
101 Acho.] om. 1639
102 come] came 1639
103 lookes_∧...see_∧]~,...~, 1639
104 oh...land!] ah...~_∧ 1639
105 stirr'd] stor'd 1639
106 Dio.] om. 1639
108 rann] run 1639
109 contradict_∧]~, 1639
112 must] much 1639; endure.]~_∧ms
113 sonne,] ~ ; 1639
114 sides,] ~ . 1639

III i

1   'Tis]_∧~ 1639
3   claime_∧...already,] ~,...~; 1639
5   Rome,] ~_∧ 1639
7   him]~, 1639
8   Nay_∧]~, 1639
10 alone,] ~_∧ 1639
15 Pure service,...declar'd;] Our~_∧...~. 1639
18 side_∧]~, 1639
20 right.] ~ ; 1639
24 souldiers,] ~_∧ 1639
26 Rome,] ~? 1639
27 fortune] fortunes 1639

29   purposes,] ~. 1639
30   hither₍ₐ₎] ~, 1639
31   ours.] ~: 1639
32   Gives] Give 1639
34   All...Gallus₍ₐ₎] Ah...~, 1639
35   and] an 1639
39   power,] ~; 1639
40   I₍ₐ₎]~, 1639
43   Cleopatra. ₍ₐ₎Twas] ~?   '~ 1639
45   has ere been heard] was ever heard ms; heard] ~; 1639
48   both] with 1639
49   fight.] ~, 1639
52   fight₍ₐ₎] ~, 1639
56   moove:] ~. 1639
57   active₍ₐ₎] ~, 1639
61   ballance,] ~; 1639
68   vaine.] ~; 1639
71   prevail'd.] ~: 1639
74   at] on 1639
75   Nay₍ₐ₎...wonder;] ~,...~, 1639
77   told.] ~: 1639
79   Canidius,] ~₍ₐ₎ 1639
81   unfought;] ~, 1639
85   yeilding₍ₐ₎] ~, 1639
86   returne;] ~. 1639
88   anger,...night.]~₍ₐ₎...~, 1639

90   time,...thinke, 's...Aegypt₍∧₎]∼₍∧₎...think's...∼. 1639
92   heart₍∧₎] ∼, 1639

III ii

s.d. Cæsar....] <u>Enter</u> Cæsar....1639

2   ₍∧₎Tis] '∼ 1639

3   cunningly₍∧₎] ∼: 1639

4   seemes₍∧₎] ∼, 1639

5   victorious₍∧₎] ∼, 1639

8   people.] ∼: 1639

12   foe₍∧₎] ∼, 1639

15   ₍∧₎twere] '∼ 1639

17   ₍∧₎Twas] '∼ 1639; intent, good] intention, ms

24   victory,] ∼; 1639

25   Herselfe,] ∼₍∧₎ 1639

27   <u>Plan</u>.] <u>Ti</u>. 1639

29   hers.] ∼; 1639

31   love letter] ∼ - ∼ 1639

32   first₍∧₎] ∼, 1639

34   that] the ms

38   Ile.] ∼; 1639

44   himselfe....all,] ∼:... ∼₍∧₎ 1639

45   presence₍∧₎] ∼, 1639

46   <u>Lucilius</u>,] ∼₍∧₎ 1639

51   Pla....carry'd!] om. 1639
52   Cæs.] om. 1639
53   Agrippa. ... Cæsar!] ~, ...~. 1639; s.d. They retire.] om. ms
56   favour,] ~ₐ 1639
57   goldₐ] ~. 1639; Plutarch.] om. ms
58   ₐTis...enough;] '~ ... ~, 1639
62   gold;] ~, 1639
66   subtlety.] ~: 1639
67   backe.] ~; 1639
75   slave.] ~: 1639
79   it.] ~, 1639
80   hither.] ~; 1639
83   confident.] ~: 1639
87   beauty....wise,] ~,...~ₐ 1639
88   instructions.] ~; 1639
89   doubt;] ~, 1639
91   face.] ~; 1639
93   hand.] ~: 1639
95   it....reply.] ~:...~ₐ 1639
96   hearty] om. ms
97   Cleopatra.] ~; 1639
101 s.d. Epa. & Eup.] om. ms
105 loyalty.] ~, 1639
106 assault. ₐTis] ~; '~1639

107 fortunes] fortune 1639
110 Eup.] Epa. 1639

III iii

1   Gallimahi Epigr. de Timone] Callimachus ms
3   mee;] ∼, 1639
5   ah] oh 1639
7   false.] ∼; 1639
10 fond] forced 1639
12 nature....Timon.] ∼:...∼, 1639
15 enough;] ∼, 1639
16 sitts;] ∼, 1639
23 teares?] ∼. 1639
27 man,] ∼; 1639
28 thee∧ Timon.... ∧tis] ∼, ∼;...'∼ 1639
30 welcome....Ist] ∼,...I'st 1639
34 belov'd,] ∼; 1639
37 thinke better] better think 1639
39 once∧] ∼, 1639
40 themselves.] ∼, 1639
41 farre; ∧twill] ∼, '∼ 1639; moe.]∼∧ms; ∼, 1639
42 wonder∧ Timon∧] ∼,∼, 1639
44 didst] did'st 1639
46 thinkst] think'st 1639
47 come;] ∼, 1639

50 hangman?] ~; 1639

51 an] on 1639

57 For] (For ms; <u>Antonius</u>~] ~, 1639

59 soule~] ~, 1639

60 <u>Ari</u>.] <u>An</u>. 1639

61 Rome~] ~, 1639

62 <u>Ari</u>....indeed;] <u>An</u>...~, 1639

63 deedes~] ~, 1639

64 consciences~] ~, 1639

68 men.] ~; 1639

69 ~Twas well~] '~~, 1639

72 was, forsooth,] ~~ ~~ 1639

73 him.] ~, 1639

74 serv'd.] ~: 1639

77 true;] ~, 1639

78 side;] ~, 1639

82 man;] ~: 1639

83 enough.] ~ ; 1639

84 appeare.] ~ ; 1639; appeare. But] appeare. <u>Ari</u>. But ms

85 <u>Ari</u>.] <u>om</u>. ms

86 slaughter!] ~. 1639

87 Oh~] ~, 1639

91 conceit,] ~~ 1639

92 newes~ ...bring~]~,...~, 1639

93 reason,] ~~ 1639

94   soe,] ~ₐ 1639;   Canidius] my Lord ms
96   fitt.] ~ ; 1639
99   slipperyₐ]~, 1639; favours,]~; ms
100 soule!] ~? 1639
101 foundationₐ]~, 1639
103 of] in 1639
106 Dooₐ] ~, 1639; Canidius]   my Lord ms
111 body.] ~: 1639
113 Yesₐ yes,] ~,~;   1639
114 here.] ~, 1639
115 I must needs preferre] fitt for that employment ms
116 Well...art.] Master of th' art.   Come Mardio. Mar. My businesse ms
117 Come...businesse] Is not to you. Ari. Marke him but well, and tell mee ms
118 you.] ~; 1639
120 Pallaceₐ] ~, 1639
121 pines.] ~, 1639
123 Ha,] ~! 1639
124 thatₐ...is't] ~,...i'st 1639; Lord.] ~: ms
128 pin'd,...sʳ?]~ₐ...Sir, 1639
131 no,] ~ₐ 1639
135 Mardioₐ] ~, 1639
136 Antonius....us!] ~?...~? 1639
137 newes,] ~ₐ 1639

139 Cæsar,] ~. 1639
140 kings.] ~; 1639
143 passion.] ~; ms
145 yett?] ~! 1639
148 Oh] ~, 1639
149 frends,] ~. 1639
153 malice;] ~, 1639
154 spirits] ~, 1639

IV i

1   kill,] ~ 1639
3   slow,] ~ 1639
6   quicke,] ~ 1639
9   suddaine...death,] ~,... ~ 1639
14 desire.] ~; 1639
16 quicke] ~, 1639
17 Well,] ~ 1639
21 Nought but that] that alone ms; happy.] ~, 1639
22 Frees...fall'n] Can cure a ruin'd fortune ms
25 cruelty.] ~, 1639
26 This...preservative] That...~, 1639
27 Controll...redeem] om. ms
28 A wofull] Redeeme a ms
29 gentle:] ~; 1639

30 so₀]∼, 1639
31 propps.] ∼: 1639
37 Queene₀]∼, 1639; Dio.] om. ms
38 Plutarch] om. ms
39 us.] ∼ ; 1639
44 willingly₀ ...Queene,] ∼ ,...∼; 1639
45 lotts₀ Mardio,] ∼ ,∼; 1639
47 fate.] ∼ : 1639
48 thee.] ∼ ; 1639
49 dead.] ∼ : 1639
51 downe,] ∼ ? 1639
55 more.] ∼ , 1639
59 Cleopatraes] Cleopatrae's 1639
60 resolv'd.] ∼ ; 1639
66 envy'd₀]∼, 1639
67 thee;] ∼, 1639
68 thence] hence 1639
70 trust.] ∼ , 1639
77 distrust₀] ∼, 1639
83 temper....young,] ∼,...∼; 1639
87 Cæsar,] ∼; 1639
90 were gratiously] were more gratiously 1639
92 frendshipp.] ∼; 1639
95 will?] ∼. 1639
96 wishes₀ ...Cleopatra₀] ∼,...∼, 1639
99 you₀ ...Queene;] ∼,...∼. 1639

100   Thyreus,] ~ₐ 1639

103   thoughtsₐ] ~, 1639

104   wishes.] ~: 1639

112   losses,] ~ₐ 1639

117   loveₐ] ~, 1639

125   love.] ~, 1639

128   perfectionsₐ] ~, 1639

129   spiritt,] ~: 1639

131   Queeneₐ]~, 1639; whom   that ms

133   skillfullₐ ...hand,] ~,...~; 1639

137   Cæsarₐ ...once,] ~,...~; 1639

138   meritt.] ~, 1639

141   name,] ~ₐ 1639

142   nothing greater] nought more great ms

144   loveₐ] ~, 1639

145   power...world] greatnesse which the world adores ms

146   Both...beautie] Brings such a freshnesse both of youth and beauty ms

148   love .] ~; 1639

149   better] clearely ms

152   meetes.] ~, 1639

153   smilesₐ] ~, 1639

154   Imperiall] imperious ms

157   beauty.] ~; 1639

161   pride.] ~: 1639

165   wee expect] w'expect 1639

168   for.] ~: 1639

171 I...anone] I will bee ready to attend youre highnesse.
    Exit Thyreus. ms

172 Farewell...s.d.] om. ms

174 Cæsar's] Cæsars 1639; I] wee ms

175 waite?] ~. 1639

178 ₍twixt...hopes.] '~ ...~! 1639

179 yett] But 1639

181 lord!] ~. 1639

182 embrace₍] ~, 1639

188 threatning₍] ~, 1639

189 greife₍] ~, 1639

194 happy;]~, 1639

195 side₍] ~, 1639

196 Titius,...Domitius,] ~₍...~. 1639

197 Dellius,...Hipparchus₍]~₍...~, 1639

198 mine.]~₍ ms; feast.] ~, 1639

199 freedome₍] ~: 1639

201 Let...souldiers] Come worthy frends; lett not a woman teach ms
202 To...stile] Us souldiers courage. Wee will stile oure feast ms
203 fellow-dyers.] ~: 1639

204 that.]~₍1639

205 love,]~₍ 1639

IV ii

2 Alexandria.] ~; 1639

3   Cæsar.] ∼ , 1639
6   Arius‸] ∼. 1639
8   ow.] ∼ , 1639
14 piety.] ∼: 1639
15 ow'd] ought 1639
16 his...naturall:] om....∼, 1639
18 philosopher,] ∼‸ 1639
21 Arius‸] ∼ , 1639
23 Arius‸] ∼ , 1639
25 victory‸] ∼ , 1639
26 away,] ∼‸ 1639
28 weary. ‸Tis] ∼: '∼ 1639
29 them.] ∼, 1639
31 provided,] ∼‸ 1639
32 horsemen,] ∼; 1639
44 gentle,...refresh'd‸] ∼;...∼. 1639

IV iii

s.d. Lucilius....] Enter Lucilius...1639
1   man,] ∼‸ 1639
2   still,...selfe!] ∼‸...∼? 1639
3   world!] ∼? 1639
7   Makes] Make 1639
8   liv'd,] ∼‸ 1639
10 enough.] ∼: 1639
12 strange....cursing,] ∼,...‸ 1639
13 ‸tis] '∼1639
14 Thyreus,] ∼‸ 1639

17   him;] ∼, 1639
21   see.] ∼∧1639
24   s.d. Exeunt.]   om. 1639

IV iv

9   him.] ∼; 1639
10   Alas∧] ∼,1639
11   now,] ∼∧ 1639
13   strength,]∼∧ 1639
16   service,] ∼ . 1639
18   things.] ∼; 1639
20   Sally;] ∼ , 1639
24   prison?...Yes,] ∼!...∼; 1639
26   art]   wert 1639
28   Lady....Thyreus] ∼,...om. 1639
37   wives∧] ∼, 1639
41   Thyreus,]∼∧ 1639
43   unconstancy.] ∼: 1639
51   heart....false,] ∼:...∼∧ 1639
52   sword.] ∼: 1639
54   nobler] noler ms
57   kept,] ∼∧ 1639
60   basenesse,]∼∧ 1639
61   is.   Farewell∧]∼:∼, 1639
63   mee.] ∼∧ 1639
66   false.] ∼: 1639

70   forth₍ₐ₎] ~, 1639

74   Canidius.] ~; 1639

78   grow.] ~: 1639

80   ₍ₐ₎Twixt] '~ 1639

81   dy,]~₍ₐ₎ 1639

83   ₍ₐ₎Twas] '~ 1639

84   ₍ₐ₎Tis...sure....there! Eira?] '~ ... ~:...~, . 1639

85   Madam?] ~! 1639

86   Yes₍ₐ₎ Madam,] ~, ~; 1639

87   goe....fates] ~,...fate 1639

90   s.d. Exeunt.] Exit. 1639

                    V i

1   revolted.] ~, 1639

2   lost,] ~; 1639

8   nought but this] nothing else ms

9   Cæsar:] ~ ; 1639

14   Lucilius,] ~; 1639

16   lov'd'st,] lov'dst₍ₐ₎ 1639

18   greife.] ~₍ₐ₎ 1639

22   tombe₍ₐ₎] ~, 1639

23   thus₍ₐ₎] ~, 1639

25   thee,]~; 1639

28   obey'd,]~; 1639

30   knowne₍ₐ₎] ~, 1639

33   none₍ₐ₎] ~ , 1639

36   Here,...sword.] ~₍ₐ₎... ~, 1639

38   command.]   ~ : 1639

39   faire.]   ~ ; 1639

41   Eros?] ~₍ₐ₎1639

44   examples]   ~ : 1639

46   Cleopatra₍ₐ₎] ~ , 1639

50   Thus₍ₐ₎...thee.]   ~,...~: 1639

52   hower.] ~, 1639

54   sight!] ~₍ₐ₎1639

57   newes....quickly₍ₐ₎ frends₍ₐ₎] ~,...~,~, 1639

59   Cleopatraes] Cleopatraes's   1639

V ii

1   you₍ₐ₎]~, 1639

2   Antonius:] ~; 1639

4   tombe;] ~, 1639

5   eloquence,] ~₍ₐ₎ 1639

9   thence] ~: 1639

11   Cæsar₍ₐ₎]~; 1639

13-14, s.d.   Titius,]   Tit:, ms

19   Alexander's sake;] Alexanders ~ , 1639

21   heere,] ~: 1639

23   greatnesse₍ₐ₎] ~, 1639

27	<u>Cæsar</u>~] ~ ,	1639
31	adore?] ~.	1639
32	<u>Achoreus</u>~] ~,	1639
37	fear'd,] ~~1639	
39	see,] ~.	1639
44	How~]~?	1639
45	feare....<u>Antonius,</u>] ~:...~.	1639
46	mee.]~~	1639
51	frend!]~~	1639
54	though I were] that I though me	
56	my] his ms	
57	my...I] his frendshipp) ms	
59	happinesse,] ~~	1639
64	ere, ~twill]~~ '~	1639
71	like~ ...service.]~,...~,	1639
72	~Tis] '~	1639
76	tombe~] ~,1639	
78	know.] ~;	1639
81	herselfe~] ~,	1639
82	I then] When I	1639
87	Queene.] ~:	1639
88	selfe.] ~:	1639
92	hands,] hand~	1639
95	Pallace;] ~.	1639
97	you;] ~.	1639
100	s.d. <u>Exeunt omnes</u>.] <u>Exeunt</u>.	1639

V iii

3   feare.] ~ : 1639
5   chiding.] ~ₐ 1639
7   ₐTis] '~ 1629
9   true....appeare;] ~,...~. 1639
12-13 s.d. Enter....]   Enter Cæsar, and Epaphroditus. 1639
14   dalliance!] ~? 1639
15   loveₐ] ~ , 1639
17   confidence;] ~. 1639
18   weakesse....heart.] ~,... ~ , 1639
19   shee.] ~ , 1639
20   Goddsₐ] ~. 1639
24   upp ₐ]~, 1639
25   desire.] ~ : 1639
30   long.] ~ : 1639
38   itₐ] ~, 1639
42   youₐ] ~, 1639
45   ₐ twere...great Antony] '~ ...Antonius 1639
47   mine,]~ₐ 1639
49   protection.] ~ : 1639
50   Cæsar's] Cæsars 1639
51   gave] give 1639
52   feild,] ~ₐ 1639

56   before.] ~: 1639

57   jealousyes.] ~, 1639

58   starre₀] ~, 1639

61   that.] ~: 1639

64   will] can 1639

65   Dio.] om. ms

66   Cleopatra.] ~: 1639

67   comforted.] ~; 1639

68   frendshipp.] ~: 1639

69   suspition.]~₀1639

71   houshold...diminished.]   port and state shall bee maintain'd at full ms

73   As ..and]   As best befitts her royalty. ms; state]   stare 1639

75   Of...friendship.]   Of oure entirest love .ms

79   jealousyes. .] ~: 1639

80   glance:] ~, 1639

84   well--]~₀1639

85   am.] ~, 1639

88   royalty;] ~, 1639

91   Cleopatra,]~₀ 1639

97   hand,]~₀ 1639

101 love ...you,]~;... ~.1639

104 not, Madam,]~₀~₀1639

105 performance.] ~, 1639

111 Cleopatraes]   Cleopatra's   1639

112 teares,] ~, 1639

115 mee.] ~: 1639

119 falsehood,] ~ . 1639

V iv

s.d. Agrippa....]   Enter Agrippa.... 1639

  2 charge,] ~, 1639

  9 suck'd,] ~, 1639

 11 two; Agrippa,] ~, ~, 1639

 16 sought.] ~, 1639

 17 these....Yes,] those....~, 1639

 18 Pallace.] ~ ; 1639

 19 newes?] ~, ms; s.d. Enter Epa.]   om. 1639

 24 her,] ~ ; 1639

 29 passe....Epaphroditus.] ~:...~, 1639

 31 late, ...feare,]~,...~, 1639

V v

s.d. Cleopatra...Charmio....is] Enter Cleopatra
     ... ~ ,...om. 1639

  1 day,]   ~ ; 1639

  3 honour,] ~, 1639

  5 Queene.] ~ , 1639

  9 Regall] Royall 1639

 13 dangers,] ~, 1639

14 of] off 1639

15 tell.] ~, 1639

16 s.d. Exeunt.]   Exeunt Glaucus and Mardio. 1639

17 Girles.] ~, 1639

18 you.] ~; 1639

21 lives,...Charmio,] ~∧ ... ~∧1639

22 mee.] ~ ; 1639

23 him.] ~ : 1639

24 Lord∧] ~, 1639

25 mansion∧] ~, 1639

27 liv'd.] ~; 1639

38 No, no∧ ...selfe,] ~,~,...~∧ 1639

52 these earthly parts]   this earth of mine ms

53 company,] ~: 1639

55 mansion,] ~; 1639

59 now∧] ~, 1639

63 storehouse,] ~∧ 1639

67 mee.] ~; 1639

70 liv'd∧] ~, 1639

73 common,] ~∧ 1639; s.d. Stabbs herselfe.]
    She stabs her self. 1639

73-74 s.d. Thyreus] om. 1639

76 dead;] ~ : 1639

77 beseem'd] became ms

78 Caesar∧]~, 1639

83 wish.] ~: 1639

85 thence.] ~, 1639

89	An]	A 1639
90	begs]	craves ms
92	dy'd]	sitts ms
95	shame,]	~. 1639
99	ever,]	~; 1639
102	crowne,]	~ˇ 1639
103	honour.]	~: 1639
104	Ptolomey.]	~: 1639
106	grant.]	~ˇ 1639
108	enterr'd,]	~ˇ 1639
109	fairest]	richest ms
114	sword;]	~, 1639
117	end. Advance,...frends,]	~: ~ ... ~ˇ 1639

Appendix 4.

Explanatory textual notes which discuss important emendations or refusals to emend.

I i

15 Lords,]   At several places 1639 shows substantive changes which have the effect of raising the social rank of the characters. Such revisions are probably authorial. See I i 27.

128-129 Here...mee]   The 1639 reading is preferable because it shows an effort to make the entrance of Mardio less abrupt.

I ii

13-15 But...come.]   The added lines in 1639 probably represent May's effort to make the entrance smoother.

53 prankes]   To "play pranks" seems to me more idiomatic than to "play feats," the 1639 reading. If the revision were made by the author, I think he also would have changed the verb. N. E. D. does not list either usage.

57 a wit so dull]   "Wit" more precisely locates the source of Antony's dullness than does "braine."

121 shall advance] ms; now shall raise 1639. The
1639 reading does not get at the difficulty of
the ms line. If "fancies" can "advance" a kingdom, they can surely also "raise" a kingdom, but
neither verb satisfactorily explains what fancies
can do for a kingdom's stature. The meaning of
the line is murky in either case.

172 Ti....Pla.] The consistent changes in speech
prefixes in 1639 in this line and in l. 174, 181,
182, 199, 205, and the change in the name of the
person addressed from Titius to Plancus in l. 183
could hardly be the work of a compositor or proofreader. May must have thought that the speeches
so re-assigned were more suitable to the characters.

217 th' effeminate] The slur on the manhood of the
Egyptians is more derogatory than the epithet
"vicious" in the ms and so is perhaps authorial.

II i

31 Are tane away] Preferable to "Remooved else"
for its immediate clarity; neither expression
avoids the delay in understanding brought about by
the cause of the removal not being mentioned until
the next clause.

42 Fall 'n from obedience] Because neither this

phrase nor the 1639 "revolted from thee" makes the meter regular, and because the sense is nearly similar, I have retained the ms reading.

II iii

25-26 And...comes.] The pronoun in the ms reading, "And make them frends," is intended to refer to Antony and Caesar, but the ms sentence is contructed so that the pronoun can also refer to a reunion of the estranged Octavia and Antony. The 1639 reading corrects this difficulty as well as provides an entrance cue.

68 Roman <u>Antony</u>] The reference is much clearer in 1639.

70-71 Not...houres,] The two specific references in the 1639 reading are preferable to the senseless line in the ms.

75 Without...other.] The line nearly ties up Cleopatra's argument.

III ii

50-53 I...writes] For these lines 1639 prints the following:

AGR.

I never heard of such a change as this.

>   Give me the letter. I'll peruse it now. <u>He reads</u>
>   AGRIPPA, AGR, CEASAR.   <u>they retire</u>.
>   CAES.

Here the woman writes....
The important differences are these: first, 1639
omits Plancus' comment at line 51; second, 1639
attributes to Agrippa Caesar's command for the
letter at line 52, but Agrippa could never make
such a command; third, 1639 makes into a stage
direction Caesar's call to Agrippa; fourth, it
makes into a stage direction the ms speech prefix
"Agri."; fifth, it makes into a stage direction
Agrippa's acknowledgement of Caesar's call,
"Caesar!"; and finally, it prints after the three
names the stage direction "<u>they retire</u>." The explanation for the confusion in 1639 is to be found
in the compositor's ommission of a line and in
his misunderstanding of line 53. His omission
of line 51 is best explained by the supposition
that his eye skipped over line 51 and settled on
the first word after the speech prefix "<u>Caes</u>."
of line 53, which he then began to set. Attempts
to explain the omitted line and speech prefixes
by considering what a compositor would have done
if he had set too many lines for the page (as

would have been the case if the two speech prefixes and omitted line had been included on C6) must begin with the assumption that the compositor did not do what any compositor would have done—simply carry the extra lines over to the next page. (He might, of course, have been dealing with marked off copy, but it still appears he could have made a fit since two lines are unused at the bottom of the page and some space could be gained at the top of the next page.) The compositor's treatment of line 53 was caused by his misunderstanding of the relationship between the three successive names and the stage direction "They retire." The ms does not have the stage direction, but writes the three names successively on one line, thus: Agrippa. Agri: Caesar! If we suppose that the stage direction was added by the author in the right margin of the printer's copy, the compositor then could have assumed that the three names were meant as a list of characters who were to "retire." Clearly he did not understand that there were not two characters, an Agrippa and another signified by the abbreviation "Agri:".

III iii

85 Ari.]   The speech prefix at the beginning of

1. 85 in 1639 is more sensible than in the
middle of 1. 84 in the ms because first, all of
line 84 describes Caesar and the subject
changes in line 85, and second, the words "But
now hee'll reigne alone" uttered by Antony
increase the pathos of his situation.

115-117 I...businesse]   The expansion in 1639
of Aristocrates' comment is more openly insult-
ing since it makes clearer to Mardio who has just
entered what he would be preferred for.

IV i

21-22 Nought...fall'n.]   The revision attempts,
in the use of the word "states," to elevate
Cleopatra's stature by making her personal fall
mean the fall of her nation. The revision is
superior because more is at stake than only her
fortune.

27-28 Controll...wofull]   The expansion continues
the notion of man's efforts to control fortune.

145-146 power...a]   Since the world seldom "adores"
"greatnesse," and since all of ms 1.146 describes the comparatively inconsequential matter
of Caesar's age and appearance, the reading in

1639, which puts proper attention on Caesar's stature, is superior.

171-172 attend...s.d.] The lines attempt to make Thyreus' departure less abrupt.

201-202 Let...stile] The ms reading excludes Cleopatra as one of Antony's worthy friends; therefore, while line 201 in 1639 has but four feet, the revision is preferable to the ms.

V ii

54-57 though...I] The several revisions in these lines make minor improvement. The revision of l. 54 is more forceful, the change from the third to the first person pronoun makes Caesar's comments more personal, and the repetition of the subject of the sentence in l. 57 keeps the syntax clear.

V iii

71 household...diminished.] Caesar's promise in the ms to maintain Cleopatra's "port and state... at full" is a vague and splendid promise; his promise in 1639 to not diminish her household servants is more specific but less splendid, and undoubtedly might more likely be kept.

75 best...friendship] The revisions in this line
and at lines 73 and 71 are insignificant, but
can be said to show a desire for more exact expression.

V v

52 these...parts] In the manuscript statement by
Cleopatra, "I'll leave this earth of mine,"
"earth" might be taken to mean her country. The
revision is an attempt to make the sense
clearer: her "clay," her body.

77 beseem'd] This revision, and the substitutions
of "begs" for "craves" (V v 90), "dy'd" for
"sitts" (V v 92), and "fairest" for "richest"
(V v 109) once again show the author aiming
for a more exact expression. Each revision
is a minor improvement.

Appendix 5.

A list of accidentals and variants in the 1639 edition's treatment of manuscript sentences ending within the line followed by a new sentence but no change of address. Lemmata show the manuscript form without silent alterations; the printed copies' forms are shown after the bracket.

I i

15   ruine. but,]   ruine. But
54   blossome, when]   blossome. When
72   parts. how]   parts. How
87   mee. but]   me; but
116   mend. for]   mend. For
132   her. now]   her. Now
135   so. wee'll]   so. Wee'll

I ii

13   bravery. but]   bravery, but
43   acceptance. but]   acceptance: but
79   mine. call]   mine. Call
86   modesty. These]   modesty: these
97   holds. but]   holds. But
114   wine! health]   wine. Health

119	is! no]	is, no
129	shortly. wee]	shortly. We
153	them. no]	them. No
176	vices. could]	vices; could
179	his. unlesse]	his. Unlesse
229	thoughts. no]	thoughts no
230	Lucilius. whither]	Lucilius, whither
234	Pelusium. what]	Pelusium. what

II i

5	heere. here]	here; here
8	assiting. when]	assisting, when
20	faction. now]	faction. Now
32	thee. nor]	thee; nor
33	him. his]	him, his
46	needy. his]	needy; his
57	in. briefly]	in; briefly
69	are. the]	are. The
77	selfe. besides]	self: besides
114	base. the]	base; the

II ii

5	long. the]	long; the
20	true. how]	true, how

II iii

47 farre. but]   farre: but
51 else? parted]   else; parted
54 now. doo]   now, do
64 mee? or]   me, or
93 behinde. besides]   behinde, besides
97 mee. for]   me, for
101 counsells?, and]   counsels, and
113 mee. great]   me Great

II iv

2 world? what]   world? What
29 prodigyes. an]   prodigies: an
55 fought. but]   fought: but
70 nation. was]   Nation. Was
83 it. on]   it: on
93 rest. this]   rest: this

III i

13 Antonius. before]   Antonius. Before
20 right. for]   right; for
31 ours. but]   ours: but
55 dy. the]   die. The
68 vaine. whoo]   vain; who

71 prevail'd. at]   prevail'd: at
77 told. after]   told: after

III ii

8   people. where]   people: where
29   hers. the]   hers; the
38   Ile. where]   Ile; where
44   himselfe. no]   himselfe: no
66   subtlety. you]   subtility: you
67   backe. for]   back; for
75   slave. her]   slave: her
79   it. but]   it, but
80   hither. I]   hither; I
83   confident. goe]   confident: go
87   beauty. thou]   beauty, thou
88   instructions. the] instructions; the
91   face. if]   face; it
93   hand. the]   hand: the
95   it. spare]   it: spare
96   hither. commend]   hither. Commend
97   Cleopatra. bidd]   Cleopatra; bid
98   all. what]   all. What
105 loyalty. souldiers] loyalty, souldiers
106 assault. tis]   assault; 'tis

6	thee. thou]	thee. Thou
12	nature. they]	nature: they
28	Timon. doost]	Timon; dost
30	welcome. what's]	welcome, what's
40	themselves. I'll]	themselves, I'll
50	hangman? but]	hangman; but
68	men. I]	men; I
74	serv'd. for]	serv'd: for
83	enough. in]	enough; in
84	appeare. Ari. but]	appear; but
96	fitt. it]	fit; it
105	perpetuity. but]	perpetuity· but
111	body. one]	body: One
112	passe. how]	passe. How
114	here. now]	here, now
140	kings. no]	Kings; no

IV i

2	speede. no]	speed. No
7	too. no]	too. No
14	desire. of]	desire; of
21	happy. that alone]	happy, nought but that
22	fortune. well]	fall'n. Well

31	propps. the]	props: the
33	operation. tis]	operation. Tis
39	us. in]	us; in
47	fate. now]	fate: now
48	thee. stay]	thee; stay
49	dead. feel'st]	dead: feel'st
55	more. as]	more, as
60	resolv'd/ nought]	resolvd'; nought
70	trust. one]	trust, one
83	temper. but]	temper, but
92	frendshipp. hee]	friendship; he
95	us. what's]	us. What's
104	wishes. nothing]	wishes: nothing
135	Graces. such]	Graces. Such
148	love. which]	love: which
157	beauty. but]	beautie: but
161	pride. in]	pride: in
168	for. meane]	for: mean
184	fortunes. had]	fortunes. Had
203	fellow-dyers. for]	fellow-dyers: for

IV ii

8	ow. a]	owe, a
14	piety. hee]	piety: he
28	weary. tis]	weary: 'tis

IV iii

29 them. for]   them, for

IV iii

10 enough. how]   enough: how
12 strange. hee's]   strange, he's

IV iv

28 Lady. beare]   Lady, bear
33 bestow'd? can]   bestow'd? Can
43 unconstancy. did]   unconstancre: did
51 heart. but]   heart: but
52 sword. make]   sword: make
61 is. farewell]   is: farewell
65 ours. I]   ours: I
66 false. my]   false: my
74 Canidius. dearest]   Canidius; dearest
78 grow. for]   grow: for
84 sure. within]   sure: within
87 goe. if]   go, if

V i

4   dy. you]   die. You
9   you. carry]   you. Carry
18 death. thy]   death. Thy
36 sword. performe.]   sword, perform

38	command. make]	command: make
39	dy. stand faire. youre]	die. Stand fair; your
44	examples. but]	examples: but
50	thee. unfaithfull]	thee: unfaithfull
52	hower. some]	houre, some
54	Antonius? oh]	*Antonius*? Oh
57	newes. convey]	news, convey

V ii

9	thence. for]	thence: for
45	feare. cruell]	fear: cruell
68	it. well]	it· well
78	know. speake]	know; speak
87	Queene. but]	Queen: but
88	her selfe. a]	herself: a

V iii

3	feare. my]	fear: my
9	true. yett]	true, yet
18	weakenesse. but]	weaknesse, but
28	you? doo]	you? Do
30	long. I]	long: I
49	protection. had]	protection: had
56	before. but]	before; but

61 that. but]   that; but
66 Cleopatra. gentle] Cleopatra: gentle
67 comforted. expect]   comforted; expect
68 frendshipp. doo]   friendshipp: do
79 jealousyes. no]   jealousies: no
85 am. I]   am, I
101 love. Caesar]   love; Caesar
105 performance. it]   performance, it
115 mee. but]   mee: but

V iv

15 sought. the]   sought, the
18 Pallace. lett]   Palace; let
19 Epaphroditus. what's]   Epaphroditus. What's
29 passe. oh]   passe: oh

V v

5   Queene, alas]   Queen, alas
15 tell. nor]   tell, nor
17 Girles. I]   Girles, I
18 you. in]   you; in
22 mee. I]   me; I
23 him. this]   him: this
27 liv'd. and]   liv'd; and
67 mee. farewell]   me; farewell

83	wish. sucke]	wish: suck
85	thence. and]	thence, and
103	honour. thou]	honour: thou
106	grant. with]	grant with
117	end. advance]	end: advance

Appendix 6.

Explanatory Notes.

I i

3   Cleopatraes]   May's form of the genitive is the historically correct Middle English -er.

5-6   To bee the ruine of Antonius. / Ca. To bee the pleasure of Antonius.]   The two lines exemplify the figure of repetition symploce, which combines anaphora (repetition of a word at the beginning of clauses) and epistrophe (repetition of a word at the end of clauses). (Joseph, Rhetoric in Shakespeare's Time, p. 305)

9   saddly on so merry]   The figure is a contrary. (Joseph, p. 322)

20   morality]   "Morality" probably in the sense of "moral discourse," but the word also suggests ethical wisdom and the speakers' moral endowments. (N.E.D.)

24   adulterismes]   The es plural ending is normal for the scribe who retained the final e of Middle English on many nouns and formed the plural by adding s.

35   A man not master of that temperance]   Plutarch

describes Antony's excessive revelling, his
public baiting of Dolabella, and his vices
(negligence, churlishness to suitors, and his
"ill name to intise mens wives"). (North's
Plutarch, "Antonius," pp. 7-10)

46 good nature] In the rare, obsolete moral sense
of natural goodness of character. (N.E.D.)

47 it] "It" is without an antecedent; the meaning
is that of Titius' lines I i 10-11: "Lett
Candidius / Have his owne way...."

49 If hee that did possesse it] "That" has been
used as a relative in all genders from Middle
English on, although it has been in and out of
favor. (Baugh, History of the English Language,
pp. 302-303)

53 Great Pompey's Sonne] Pompey's son was Cneus
Pompey (North's Plutarch, "Antonius," p. 25);
"Great Pompey," 106-48 b.c., formed the first
triumvirate with Julius Caesar and Crassus in
60. (Encyclopaedia Britannica, 11th ed.)

54 that family] Pompey's family; his ruin
"fill'd the world" (l. 55) because his was the
cause of "the senate and aristocracy."
(Encyclopaedia Britannica, 11th ed.)

55 was overthrowne] Julius Caesar overthrew
Pompey at Pharsalia in 48 b.c., and Pompey
was killed by one of his followers when he

sought refuge in Egypt.

62 priviledge] A privileged position. (N.E.D.)

68 Soule...witt] "Soule" as "the principle of thought and action in man," and "witt" in the archaic sense of "the faculty of thinking and reasoning in general: mental capacity." (N.E.D.)

72 parts] "Parts" in the sense of "a personal quality or attribute, natural or acquired, especially of an intellectual kind." (N.E.D.)

72-73 languages Speakes shee] "She spake unto few barbarous people by interpreter, but made them aunswere her selfe, or at the least the most parte of them: as the AEtheopians, the Arabians, the Troglodytes, the Hebrues, the Syrians, the Medes, and the Parthians, and to many others also, whose languages she had learned. Whereas diverse of her progenitors, the kings of AEgypt, could scarce learne the AEgyptian tongue only, and many of them forgot to speake the Macedonian." (North's Plutarch, "Antonius," p. 27)

74 Troglodites] "A primitive people who dwelt in...caves, mostly on the Red Sea coast south of Egypt." (Oxford Classical Dictionary)

75 Medes, and Parthians]   The Medes were inhabitants of Media, an ancient country in NW Iran (New Century Cyclopedia), and the Parthians of Parthia, a country in E Asia which Antony had tried to conquer just before the events of this play. (North's Plutarch, "Antonius")

80 Ptolemaeus Philadelphus]   The scribe does not show the genitive by apostrophe.

82 forgot the Macedonian.]   That Cleopatra's forebears had forgotten the Macedonian tongue is striking because Ptolemy I had been an officer in the army of Alexander the Great, a Macedonian. Ptolemy was awarded Egypt on the distribution of the provinces after Alexander's death. (New Century Cyclopedia)

106 That Antony and Caesar could usurpe]   The account of Antony's and Caesar's misrepresentation of the dead Caesar's wishes so that their own ends would be served is in North's Plutarch, "Antonius," p. 15.

119 Freeer]   "Free" in the obsolete sense of noble, honourable, generous. (N.E.D.)

121 Ambition]   See note for II ii 13.

124 Could]   Ellipsis of "I" before "Could..."

13 bravery⌉ Display, show, splendour. (N.E.D.)

44 freely⌉ In regard to actions, unrestrained;
but in regard to character and conduct, nobly,
honorably. (N.E.D.)

53 ere] At an earlier time. (N.E.D.)

56 transcends⌉ Excells. (N.E.D.)

71 Hannibal was charm'd at Capua] In the winter
of 216-215 b.c. while invading Italy, Hannibal
wintered at Capua, "where it was alleged...that
luxurious quarters undermined the discipline of
his troops." (Oxford Classical Dictionary)

77 His active life knew how to revell well.]
"The noble men...hate [Antony] for his
naughty life: for they did abhor his banckets
and dronken feasts he made at unseasonable
times, and his extreme wastful expences upon
vaine light huswives....In his house they did
nothing but feast, daunce, and maske." (North's
Plutarch, "Antonius," pp. 9-10)

84 Coelosyria] South Syria. (Webster's Geographical Dictionary)

100 Cyprus] An unmarked genitive; see the scribe's
similar treatment of the construction at I i 80.
The gift of kingdoms is reported in North's

Plutarch, "Antonius," p. 36.

101 ominous] Of good omens, auspicious, fortunate. (N.E.D.)

112 Cyprus ever was faire Venus Ile.] May uses the Roman name of Aphrodite, whose traditional home and temple were on Cyprus.

121 fancyes] Synonomous with imagination in May's time; "the process and the faculty, of forming mental representations of things not present to the senses." (N.E.D.)

122 Paphos] The old city of Paphos on Cyprus, in which Aphrodite's temple was located. (New Century Cyclopedia)

144 shape] Assumed appearance, guise. (N.E.D.)

157 thunderer] Jove, as in "The mighty Thund'rer [Jove] heard...' (Dryden, AEneis IV 321). May uses the Roman name for Zeus, which "signifies 'sky'...and the cults prove that Zeus is the weather-god, i.e. the sky as the sphere of...thunder." (Oxford Classical Dictionary)

171 Marcus Cato] Cato the Younger, 95-46 b.c. In 58 b.c. he undertook the "annexation of Cyprus, over which...his reputation for fairness remained unimpaired." (Oxford Classical Dictonary)

186 Artavasdes] Ruled Armenia, in W Asia, SE of
the Black Sea, c. 55-34 b.c. (New Century
Cyclopedia)

188-191 A situation analagous to Artavasdes; occurs
in Marlowe's Tamburlaine Part I when Bajazeth,
Emperor of the Turks, is made to kneel so Tamburlaine can use him as a footstool to ascend
the throne. Tamburlaine cages but does not chain
Bajazeth:

> There, while he lives, shall Bajazeth be kept,
> And where I go be there in triumph drawn.
> IV ii 85-86

193 Calvisius] "One of Caesar's friends reproved"
Antony for several faults, among them giving to
Cleopatra "all the libraries of the royall citie
of Pergamum, in the which she had above two
hundred thousand bookes." (North's Plutarch,
"Antonius," p. 61)

224 Caius Marius] See 1. 225.

225 Samnites] Ancient Italic people of Samnium
in central Italy. Wars between the Romans and
the Samnites occurred in 343-41, 328-04, and
298-90 b.c. (Oxford Classical Dictionary, New
Century Cyclopedia)

226 dotage] Excessive love or fondness. (N.E.D.)

II i

1 Tis not the place, nor marble walls that]
An echo of Shakespeare's sonnet 55, also perhaps echoed by Lovelace in stanza 4 of "To Althea, from Prison."

5 both her Consuls] "According to the traditional account...the head magistrates were two in number from the beginning." (Oxford Classical Dictionary)

7 that sacred order] The number of Roman senators differed at different periods; their number was increased from 300 to 600 by Sulla, from 600 to 900 by Julius Cæsar, and reduced to 600 by Augustus. (Oxford Classical Dictionary)

10-11 Camillus...Veii] Several times dictator, the Roman general Camillus took Veii, a city 11 miles NW of Rome, in 396 b.c. (New Century Cyclopedia)

25 rëindeniz'd] To endenize is to make a citizen of a person. (N.E.D.)

27 price] "ME pris had all the OF senses 'price. value, honour, prize, praise'; it first threw off the last of these.... During the last 300 years it has also thrown off the fourth sense, for

which the by form <u>prize</u> has been established."
(<u>N.E.D</u>.) The 1639 edition spells the word "prize."
See III i 46. The 1639 edition of May's tragedy
<u>Agrippina</u> spells both "price" and "prize:"

> Nor doe wee price our name <u>Britannicus</u>
> Fetch'd from that Iland, lesse then <u>Scipio</u>
> His honour'd name of <u>Africanus</u> priz'd. (1.619-621)

60-63 Comagena...Galatia] All the countries are in the eastern Mediterranean, the area of <u>Antony's</u> rule.

66   talent] The value of a talent weight; the weight varied greatly. (<u>N.E.D</u>.)

67   freely] Generously, nobly; also, of an act, done of one's own accord. (<u>N.E.D</u>.)

112   <u>Cæsar</u> much] Elision of "so": "favors <u>Cæsar</u> [so] much."

116   moile] A current spelling of "mule;" in the 1639 edition spelled "moyle."

II ii

13   ambition] Traditionally an error of the great, near-allied to pride. Of Julius Cæsar, Plutarch says, "Nothing els moved him to make warre with all the world...but one selfe cause, which first procured Alexander and Cyrus before

him: to wit, an insatiable desire to raigne, with
a senseles covetousnes to be the best man in
the world." (North's <u>Plutarch</u>, "Antonius,"
p. 7)

18 associate] In the obsolete sense of accompany.
(<u>N</u>.<u>E</u>.<u>D</u>.)

25 certainty] A fact or thing certain or sure.
(<u>N</u>.<u>E</u>.<u>D</u>.)

27 order may be taken.] "To take order" in the
obsolete sense of "to take measures or steps."
(<u>N</u>.<u>E</u>.<u>D</u>.)

II iii

2 use moe circumstances] "To furnish with details,
set forth with attendant circumstances."
Obsolete. (<u>N</u>.<u>E</u>.<u>D</u>.)

6 maugre] The archaic adverb meaning "notwithstanding, in spite of." (<u>N</u>.<u>E</u>.<u>D</u>.)

24 as once before shee did] When Antony and
Cæsar quarreled, Octavia, Cæsar's sister and
Antony's wife, though with child, journeyed to
reconcile them. "Shee tooke them aside, and
with all the instance she could possible, in-
treated them they would not suffer her that was

the happiest woman of the world, to become nowe
the most wretched." (North's Plutarch, "Antonius,"
pp. 35-36)

30 effects] In the obsolete sense of "something
which is.. acquired by action." (N.E.D.)

38-39 beare you company] To accompany. (N.E.D.)

48 Distast] "To displease, offend;" now rare, but
frequent in the seventeenth c. (N.E.D.)

66 wretched] "Living in a state of misery, poverty,
or degradation." (N.E.D.)

79-80 recreate] As a reflexive verb, "to refresh
oneself with some agreeable occupation or pastime."
(N.E.D.)

109 Bellona] The Roman war-goddess. (Oxford Classical
Dictionary)

111 cohorts] "A body of infantry in the Roman army,
of which there were ten in a legion, each
consisting of from 300-600 men." (N.E.D.)

II iv

3 prodigious] "Of the nature of a prodigy...
portentous." Obsolete. (N.E.D.) Signs and
portents other than those in the play are reported
in North's Plutarch, "Antonius," p. 63, but those
in the play are from Dio Cassius, Bk. 50, pp.
276-277.

6   Chaos...involve]   "Chaos" meant "the cosmic
    anarchy before creation and the wholesale
    dissolution that would result if the pressure
    of Providence relaxed." (Tillyard, Elizabethan
    World Picture, p. 16) To "involve" is "to
    envelop within the folds of some condition or
    circumstance." (N.E.D.)

15 adamantine]   Immovable, impregnable; the
    noun "adamant" was used poetically for "anything
    very hard and indestructible." (N.E.D.)

16 banefull]   Destructive to well being. (N.E.D.)

22 firmament]   The sky or heavens, but perhaps,
    as in the old astronomy, the sphere containing
    the fixed stars; the eighth heaven of the Ptolemaic
    system. (N.E.D.)

30 the house of Concord]   The house was built and
    rebuilt three times, and "stood in an elevated
    position at the west end of the Forum." (Oxford
    Companion to Classical Literature, pp. 119-120)

32 the people's Genius]   By "genius" was meant
    "the attendant spirit allotted to every person
    at his birth, to govern his fortunes and
    determine his character." (N.E.D.) But "we
    hear also of a Genius populi Romani, and a Genius

urbis ^{R}omae" (Oxford Companion to Classical Literature), so the notion of a personal attendant spirit was broadened.

35 mount Aventine] The southermost of the seven hills of ancient Rome. (New Century Cyclopedia)

36 Victoriaes image on the theater] Victoria was the Roman equivalent of Greek Nike, the goddess of victory, whose "temple on the Palatine dates from 294 b.c.," and whose image was found about Rome. (Oxford Classical Dictionary)

44 corne] Grain. (N.E.D.)

45 Etruria] A part of ancient Italy now modern Tuscany.

110 skill] Although the construction is slightly different here, the meaning is that of the phrase "can skill, to have...knowledge, esp. in a specified matter." (N.E.D.)

III i

15 now they have declar'd] The gods favored the victors; even in Richard II heaven was believed to be the judge of the trial by combat. (Richard II, I ii 6; I iii 110)

36 Paraetonium] Now Matrûh, a village 150 miles from Alexandria. (Webster's Geographical Dictionary)

48 the fleetes encountred both] In apposition
with a plural noun, "when referring to the subject
of a sentence, both was in early ME usually
separated from it, and placed after the verb or
whole predication. This is still common
dialectically." (N.E.D.)

69 made good the navall fight] "To gain and hold
one's ground, a position." (N.E.D.)

91 Pelusium] An ancient city at the NE extremity
of the Nile delta; its ruins are about 22 miles
SE of Port Said, on the Bay of Pelusium, an inlet
of the Mediterranean. (Webster's Geographical
Dictionary)

III ii

10 Parthian king] See I i 75.

14 basely had surprisd] Antony lured Artavasdes,
who on the Parthian expedition had deserted with
his troops, to Egypt and there imprisoned him.
(North's Plutarch, "Antonius," pp. 38, 39, 53)

27 Brave and ominous] Brave: "an indeterminate word,
used to express the superabundance of any
valuable quality in men or things." Archaic.

(Johnson, quoted in N.E.D.) Ominous: portentous, either auspicious or inauspicious. (N.E.D.)

38   Pharos Ile...Timon] Pharos was "opposite ancient Alexandria, on which Ptolemy I and II erected a celebrated lighthouse, one of the wonders of the ancient world." (New Century Cyclopedia) Timon lived in Athens in the fifth century.

48   doubt] Suspect; archaic. (N.E.D.)

55   gratify my favour] "To make a present (usually of money)...esp. as a reward...or as a bribe." (N.E.D.)

83   fellow] A "customary title of address to a servant or other person of humble station" not, in Shakespeare, contemptuously used unless applied to one not greatly inferior. Obsolete. (N.E.D.)

III iii

s.d. and ff.   The story of Antony as Timon, with the epigraph by Callimachus, is in North's Plutarch, "Antonius," pp. 73-74.

10   fond] Foolish, silly. (N.E.D.)

24   foolish] "Fool-like; wanting in sense or judgement." (N.E.D.)

52   good parts and gravity] Part: "a personal quality or attribute, natural or acquired, esp.

of an intellectual kind." Gravity: "weight,
influence, authority." (N.E.D.)

69 carefully] Ellipsis: "carefully [done]."

71 Cicero] After the murder of Julius Caesar,
Cicero "pronounced the Philippics in 44 and 43
against Antony, whom he detested, for which he
was proscribed by the Second Triumvirate...and
slain in 43." (New Century Cyclopedia) When
the executioners brought Antony Cicero's head
and hand, Plutarch reports that Antony "beheld
them a long time with great joy, and laughed
heartily." (North's Plutarch, "Antonius," p. 19)

77 Catiline's plott] In 64 b.c., Catiline "organized
a widespread conspiracy against the republic...which
was defeated by the vigilance and eloquence
of Cicero." (New Century Cyclopedia)

81 his father] Augustus Caesar was the son of Caius
Ocatvius, who had "governed Macedonia with conspi-
cuous ability" and rose to the praetorship. (Oxford
Classical Dictionary)

82 do reason] The phrase "to do reason" means
"that treatment which may with reason be expected
by, or required from, a person." Obsolete. (N.E.D.)

88 shape] Assumed appearance. (N.E.D.)

99   Fortunes slippery and unconstant favours] Lydgate
     speaks of "fals Fortune" in the <u>Fall of Princes</u>,
     and the idea of the fickleness of fortune, one of the
     agents by which God obtained His effects in the
     world (the other agents were Providence, Hap, and
     Chance) is a commonplace in medieval and Renaissance
     literature, found, for example, in Boccaccio, <u>De
     Casibus</u>, Chaucer, <u>Monk's Tale</u> and the <u>Mirror for
     Magistrates</u>.

110 kill upp]   "To get rid of (a number, a whole tribe)
     by killing." Obsolete.   (<u>N.E.D</u>.)

125 constitution of her body]   The "physical nature of
     character of the body in regard to healthiness,
     strength." (<u>N.E.D</u>.)

143 It makes a deepe impression in his passion]   The
     emotions as distinguished from reason; the passions
     resided in the appetitive part of the sensible soul
     and so were "the potential enemy of the rational
     soul." (Campbell, <u>Shakespeare's Tragic Heroes</u>,
     pp. 68, 78)

152 Meroë]   The name "for the region bounded on three
     sides by the Nile...the Atbara..., and the Blue
     Nile; and the special name of an ancient city on the
     east bank of the Nile." (<u>Encyclopedia Britannica</u>,
     11th ed.)

IV i

18   adventure]   Figuratively, to dare to undertake. (<u>N.E.D</u>.)

19 still] As an adverb, now obsolete, "sometimes used where the comparative notion is merely implied." (N.E.D.)

34 Cleopatra's experiments are not made in the spirit of Bacon; her activities are described in detail by Plutarch, "Antonius," p. 75.

62 worm] Archaic for serpent. (N.E.D.)

63 rate] Economic imagery is common in Elizabethan poetry; see Shakespeare's sonnet 146, and Merchant of Venice, III ii 111-113, 141-169, where Bassanio and Portia declare their love in such imagery.

73 madd Octavia] In Plutarch she is beautiful, well-mannered, intelligent, and noble.

83 temper] "Habitual disposition" as well as "actual state or attitude of the mind or feelings." (N.E.D.)

100 meanest] In the obsolete sense about the rank of persons, of low degree. (N.E.D.)

122 rude] Unexpert, unskilled. Archaic. (N.E.D.)

141 the triple world] Probably the three continents of Africa, Asia, and Europe.

199 freedome] "The overstepping of...customary bounds of speech or behavior." (N.E.D.)

IV ii

16-17 naturall...mentall] Matters of the body as opposed to matters of the mind.

IV iii

2   Queene of this little world]   "Therefore was man called microcosmos, or, the little world." (Raleigh, quoted in T. Spencer, Shakespeare and the Nature of Man, p. 20) The soul was queen of the "little world" because it was believed to have the three controlling powers of "lyfe vegitable," "life sensible," and "solle reasonable." (John Wilkinson's 1547 translation of Aristotle's Ethics, quoted in Campbell, Shakespeare's Tragic Heroes, p. 64)

7   offer at]   To make an attempt at. Now rare or obs. (N.E.D.)

17 carryes it so plainely]   Without concealment. (N.E.D.)

23 Hands on]   To "lay hands on." Obsolete. (N.E.D.)

56 nor...nor]   "A negative conjunction introducing both alternatives, chiefly poetic." (N.E.D.)

61 approve]   To show to be true, prove. Obsolete. (N.E.D.)

79 past]   An alternate spelling of "passed." (N.E.D.)

V i

12 glasse]   A sand-glass, for the measurement of time. (N.E.D.)

13 expects a period]   Consummation or end. (N.E.D.)

22-35 Antony's farewell to the world and his occupation, a conventional speech by the hero before his death. See Othello, III iii 347-357, and Antony and Cleopatra,

IV sii 18-29.

Of thy proud wheele] Fortune was depicted in the middle Ages and Renaissance as a goddess who governed the turning of a wheel on which clutched those who were rising or falling in her favor. See the illustrations in Campbell, Shakespeare's Tragic Heroes, pp. 4-5.

Zones] The five "encircling regions...into which the surface of the earth...is divided by the tropics... and the polar vircles." (N.E.D.)

usher...Elisian feilds] An "usher" is "one who precedes or arrives before another, esp. a higher dignitary." (N.E.D.) Elysium, first conceived as the Isles of the Blest at the ends of the earth where "favored heroes, exempted from death, were translated by the gods" was, in a later age, "transferred to the nether regions." (Oxford Classical Dictionary)

unfaithfull faithfull] The figure is an immediate contrary. (Joseph, Rhetoric in Shakespeare's Time, p. 322.)

Too kindely cruell, falsely vertuous] An ellipsis of subject and verb (you are), unless the question mark in the preceding line is regarded as "rhetorical" only, signifying a comma. The figure is, strictly, scesia onomaton, made up of only substantive and adjective. (Joseph, p. 296) Each pair of adjectives and substantives is a contradictory term. (Joseph,

p. 323) Finally, lines 41-42 represent homoioteleuton, combined with isocolon and alliteration. Homoioteleuton "accentuates the rhythm of the equal members by its own similar endings," (Joseph, p. 298) and isocolon "'maketh the members...to be almost of a just number of sillables.'" (Peacham, quoted in Joseph, p. 297)

48 where nor time nor death] The negative conjunction used to introduce two alternatives. (N.E.D.)

V ii

14 palenesse of youre feare] Of a person, a "whitish or ashen appearance...temporarily as a result of fear." (N.E.D.)

34 hearse] A corpse. (N.E.D.)

47 white a day] The now rare meaning of a fortunate, happy day. (N.E.D.)

76 lett upp] Raised. (N.E.D.)

83 held her talke] The phrase is not in N.E.D., but the meaning is clear from the context: engaged. her in conversation.

93 spake her faire] Addressed her courteously. (N.E.D.)

98 admit] Receive. (N.E.D.)

V iii

19 faire] Beautiful. (N.E.D.)

30 These many yeares] So many years as I shall now describe.

31 Worthy] An anachronism. One of the nine famous personages of ancient and medieval history and legend; 3 Jews, Joshua, David and Judas Maccabæus; 3 Gentiles, Hector, Alexander, and Julius Cæsar; 3 Christians, Arthur, Charlemagne, and Godfrey of Bouillon. (N.E.D.)

34 his Sonne] "Octavius Cæsar the younger came to Rome, who was the sonne of Julius Cæsar's nece... and was left his lawfull heire by will." (North's Plutarch, "Antonius," p. 15) Dio Cassius, however, says that "Cleopatra had envolved Octavius' father." (Bk. 51, p. 322) and he has Cleopatra say to Octavius about a picture, "you see with your own eyes your father in the guise in which he often visited me." (Bk. 51, p. 326.)

46 favours] Instances of exceptional kindness. (N.E.D.)

49 share of rule] The triumvirate divided the world so that Lepidus received Africa, Octavius all the lands west of the Ionian Sea and Antony all east of the Ionian Sea.

52 Cassius] Cassius and Brutus were defeated at Philippi by Antony and Octavius 42 b.c.

54 as false as truth it selfe is true] The
figure of repetition ploce, "the speedy iteration
of one word at frequent intervals," (Joseph, pp.
306-307) and alliteration.

56 Cilicia] An ancient country in SE Asia
Minor, now in modern Turkey. (<u>Webster's</u> <u>Geographical</u>
<u>Dictionary</u>)

78 overreach] Overpower; obs. (<u>N.E.D</u>.)

87 unexampled] Unparalleled. (<u>N.E.D</u>.)

119 <u>Ariadne</u> pardons <u>Theseus</u> falsehood] Theseus
forgot and left Ariadne on Naxos after fleeing
with her from the Labyrinth. (<u>Oxford</u> <u>Classical</u>
<u>Dictionary</u>)

120 <u>Dido</u>] AEneid Books III-IV tells the Dido and
Æneas story.

121 <u>Troilus</u>] The Troilus story is told by Boccaccio,
Chaucer, and Shakespeare. This is the only
one of the three allusions in lines 119-121 in which
the female is false.

V iv

s.d. Psylls] While the noun is not recorded in N.E.D.,
the rare adjective "Psyllic" means "of or pertain-
ing to snake-charming," from Greek "Psylloi,"

Latin "Psylli," and "African people, famed as snake charmers." (N.E.D.) The Psylli are described by Dio Cassius, Bk. 51, p. 329.

2 gave in charge] Commanded. (N.E.D.)

8 his] The normal possessive neuter pronoun until about 1600, when "it's" (spelled with an apostrophe until about 1800) began gradually to replace it. (Baugh, History of the English Language, pp. 300-302)

9 Aesculapius] The Greek God of Medicine.

17 Carry them] "To...lead a person with one...to a place." (N.E.D.)

24 neerly] Particularly. (N.E.D.)

V v

3 magnificence] "As the name of one of the 'moral virtues'...liberality of expenditure combined with good taste." (N.E.D.)

4 pompous] "Characterized by pomp or stately show." (N.E.D.)

7 Destinyes] "The three goddesses held, in Greek and Roman mythology, to determine the course of human life." (N.E.D.)

54 dissolve togither] A "melting" image echoing the many in Shakespeare's Antony and Cleopatra:

>   As it determines, so
> Dissolve my life! The next Caesarion smite!
> Till by degrees the memory of my womb,
> Together with my brave Egyptians all,
> By the discandying of this pelleted storm
> Lie graveless....   III xiii 161-166

See also <u>Antony and Cleopatra</u> IV viii 20, IV xii 22, IV xiv 24, and IV xv 63 for other "melting" images.

61   common elements] The phrase is not in <u>N.E.D</u>. The four elements of ancient chemistry were earth, water, air, and fire; "common" probably signifies that the elements are common to all men. Since "common" also means "of ordinary occurrence... hency mean, cheap" (<u>N.E.D</u>.),Cleopatra probably suggests that her flesh is less important than her spirit.

63   pos'd] Puzzled, confused. (<u>N.E.D</u>.)

69   spleene] Hot or proud temper; obsolete. (<u>N.E.D</u>.)

87   exorable] "Capable of being moved by entreaty." (<u>N.E.D</u>.)

94   Had feeble <u>Perseus</u> knowne so brave a course] Brave: stouthearted. Perseus was the last king of Macedonia who in a war with Rome was defeated by Aemilius Paulus in 168 b.c., was dethroned, and taken captive to Rome in 167. (<u>New Century Cyclopedia</u>)

104 race of Ptolemy] The dynasty ruled Egypt from
323 b.c. to Cleopatra's death in 30 b.c. (<u>Encyclopædia</u>
<u>Britannica</u>, 11th ed.)

107 Memphis] An ancient city in Lower Egypt,
traditionally the capitol of most of the rulers
of Egypt to Alexander the Great. (<u>Webster's</u>
<u>Geographical</u> <u>Dictionary</u>)

114 civil] Of or belonging to citizens. (<u>N</u>.<u>E</u>.<u>D</u>.)

118 Eagles] "A figure of the bird used...as an
ensign in the Roman army." (<u>N</u>.<u>E</u>.<u>D</u>.)

LIST OF WORKS CITED

Barnhart, Clarence L., et al., eds. The New Century Cyclopedia of Names. 3 vols. New York: Appleton-Century-Crofts, 1954.

Baugh, Albert. A History of the English Language. New York: Appleton-Century Co., 1935.

Bennett, H.S. Chaucer and the Fifteenth Century. New York: Oxford University Press, 1947.

Bentley, G. E. The Jacobean and Caroline Stage. 5 vols. Oxford: Oxford University Press, 1956.

Bladon, James. "Thomas May's Tragedy of Agrippina." Notes and Queries, 4th Series, II (1868), 132.

Boas, F.S. The Works of Thomas Kyd. Oxford: The Clarendon Press, 1901.

Boccaccio, Giovanni. Concerning Famous Women. Trans. Guido A. Guarino. New Brunswick, N.J.: Rutgers University Press, 1963.

Bowers, Fredson. "Current Theories of Copy-Text, with an Illustration from Dryden." Modern Philology, XLVIII (1950), 12-20.

-----, ed. The Dramatic Works of Thomas Dekker. 4 vols. (Cambridge, England: Cambridge University Press, 1953-1961.

-----. "Elizabethan Proofing." In J. Q. Adams Memorial Studies. Ed. J. G. McManaway. Washington, D.C.: Folger Shakespeare Library, 1948. Pp. 571-586.

Bowers, Fredson. "Established Texts and Definitive Editions." <u>Philological Quarterly</u>, XLI (1962), 1-17.

-----. "Notes on Running Titles as Bibliographical Evidence." <u>The Library</u>, 4th Series, XIX (1938), 315-338.

-----. "Old Spelling Editions of Dramatic Texts." In <u>Studies in Honor of T. W. Baldwin</u>. Ed. Don C. Allen. Urbana, Illinois: University of Illinois Press, 1958. pp. 9-15.

-----, ed. <u>On Editing Shakespeare and the Elizabethan Dramatists</u>. Philadelphia: University of Pennsylvania Library, 1955.

-----. <u>Textual and Literary Criticism</u>. Cambridge, England: Cambridge University Press, 1959.

-----. "Textual Criticism." In <u>The Aims and Methods of Scholarship in Modern Languages and Literatures</u>. Ed. James Thorpe. New York: The Modern Language Association, 1963. Pp. 23-42.

Briggs, W. D. "The Influence of Jonson's Tragedy in the Seventeenth Century." <u>Anglia</u>, XXV (1912), 277-337.

Brown, Arthur. "The Rationale of Old-Spelling Editions of the Plays of Shakespeare and his Contemporaries: A Rejoinder." <u>Studies in Bibliography</u>, XIII (1960), 69-76.

Brown, John Russell. "The Rationale of Old-Spelling Editions of the Plays of Shakespeare and his Contemporaries." Studies in Bibliography, XIII (1960), 49-68.

Bruère, R. T. "The Latin and English Versions of Thomas May's Supplementum Lucani." Classical Philology, XLIV (1949), 145-163.

Campbell, Lily B. Shakespeare's Tragic Heroes: Slaves of Passion. New York: Barnes and Noble, 1961.

Cary, Max, et al., eds. The Oxford Classical Dictionary. Oxford: The Clarendon Press, 1949.

Chester, A. G. Thomas May: Man of Letters, 1595-1650. Philadelphia: University of Pennsylvania, 1932.

Cranfill, Thomas M., ed. Rich's Farewell to Military Profession 1581. Austin: University of Texas, 1959.

Danby, John F. Poets on Fortune's Hill. London: Faber and Faber, 1952.

Daniel, Samuel. The Complete Works in Verse and Prose of Samuel Daniel. Ed. Alexander B. Grosart. 5 vols. London: 1885-1896.

Dio Cassius. Dio's Rome. Trans. Herbert B. Foster. 6 vols. Troy, New York: Pafraets Book Co., 1906.

Ellis-Fermor, Una. *Jacobean Drama: An Interpretation*. 4th ed. London: Methuen and Co., 1961.

The Encyclopædia Britannica. 11th ed. New York: Encyclopædia Britannica Co., 1910-1911.

Florus, Lucius Annaeus. *Epitome of Roman History*. Trans. Edward S. Forster. London: Heinemann, 1929.

Furness, H. H., ed. *The Tragedie of Anthonie and Cleopatra*. In *A New Variorum Edition of Shakespeare*. 22 vols. Philadelphia: J. B. Lippincott Co., 1871-1939. Vol. 15, 1907.

Gower, John. *The English Works of John Gower*. Ed. G. C. Macaulay. 2 vols. In Early English Text Society, Extra Series, No. 81-82. London: K. Paul, Trench, Trübner and Co., 1900-1901.

Greg, W. W. *A Bibliography of the English Printed Drama to the Restoration*. 4 vols. London: Oxford University Press, 1939-1959.

-----. *The Editorial Problem in Shakespeare*. Oxford: Oxford University Press, 1942.

-----. "An Elizabethan Printer and His Copy." *The Library*, 4th Series, IV (1924), 102-118.

-----, ed. *English Literary Autographs 1550-1650*. 3 vols. and suppl. London: Oxford University Press, 1925-1932.

-----. "The Rationale of Copy-Text." *Studies in Bibliography*, III (1950), 19-36.

-----. *The Variants in the First Quarto of King Lear*:

A Bibliographical and Critical Inquiry. London: Oxford University Press, 1940.

Harbage, Alfred. Annals of English Drama, 975-1700. Philadelphia: University of Pennsylvania Press, 1940.

Harington, John. Nugæ Antiquæ. Ed. Henry Harington. 2 vols. London: Vernor and Hood, 1804.

Harvey, Paul, ed. The Oxford Companion to Classical Literature. Oxford: The Clarendon Press, 1955.

Hinman, Charlton. "Principles Governing the Use of Variant Spellings as Evidence of Alternate Setting by Two Compositors." The Library, 4th Series, XXI (1940), 78-94.

Howard, Edwin J., ed. Of the Knowledge Which Maketh a Wise Man. By Sir Thomas Elyot, Oxford, Ohio: The Anchor Press, 1946.

Knights, L.C. Drama and Society in the Age of Jonson. London: Chatto and Windus, 1951.

Lee, Sidney L., ed. The Autobiography of Edward, Lord Herbert of Cherbury. London: John C. Nimms, 1886.

Lydgate, John. Lydgate's Fall of Princes. Ed. Henry Bergen. 4 vols. Washington, D.C.: The Carnegie Institution of Washington, 1923.

MacCallum, M. W. *Shakespeare's Roman Plays*. London: Macmillan and Co., 1910.

The Malone Society. "Rules for the Guidance of Editors of the Society's Reprints." In *Collections* I.2, The Malone Society. Oxford: 1908.

-----. "Rules for the Guidance of Editors of the Society's Reprints." In *Collections* IV, The Malone Society. Oxford: 1956, CIII, 66-69.

Marlowe, Christopher. *Tamburlaine the Great*. Ed. U. M. Ellis-Fermor. London: Methuen and Co., 1930.

McKerrow, Ronald B. *An Introduction to Bibliography for Literary Students*. Oxford: Oxford University Press, 1927.

-----. *Prolegomena for the Oxford Shakespeare*. Oxford: The Clarendon Press, 1939.

-----, ed. *The Works of Thomas Nashe*. 5 vols. London: Sidgwick and Jackson, 1904-1910.

Murray, James A. H., ed. *A New English Dictionary on Historical Principles*. 10 vols. in 20. Oxford: The Clarendon Press, 1888-1928.

Plutarch's Lives of the Noble Grecians and Romans. Trans. Sir Thomas North. 6 vols. London: David Nutt, 1895-1896.

Pollard, A. W., and G. R. Redgrave. *A Short-Title Catalogue of Books Printed in England, Scotland, and of English Books Printed Abroad 1475-1640*. London: The Bibliographical Society, 1926.

Robinson, F. N., ed. *The Works of Geoffrey Chaucer*. 2nd ed. Boston: Houghton Mifflin Co., 1957.

Rollins, Hyder E., and Herschel Baker, eds. *The Renaissance in England: Non-Dramatic Prose and Verse of the Sixteenth Century*. Boston: D. C. Heath and Co., 1954.

Salingar, L. G. "The Decline of Tragedy." *The Age of Shakespeare*, in *A Guide to English Literature*. 7 vols. Penguin Books, 1955, II, 429-440.

Schmid, F. E., ed. *The Tragedy of Julia Agrippina, Empresse of Rome*. In *Materialien zur Kunde des älteren Englischen Dramas*, XLIII. Ed. W. Bang. Louvain: A. Uystpruyst, 1914.

Sensebaugh, G. P. *The Tragic Muse of John Ford*. Stanford, California: Stanford University Press, 1944.

Sister M. Simplicia Fitzgibbons, ed. *The Old Couple*, by Thomas May. Washington, D.C.: Catholic University of America Press, 1943.

Sister Mary Ransom Burke, ed. *The Tragedy of Cleopatra, Queen of Aegypt, Edited, with an Introduction*. Unpublished Ph.D. thesis, Fordham, 1943.

Sister Miriam Joseph. *Rhetoric in Shakespeare's Time*. New York: Harcourt, Brace and Co., 1962.

Spencer, Theodor. *Shakespeare and the Nature of Man*. New York: Macmillan, 1942.

Steele, Mary S. *Plays and Masques at Court*. New Haven: Yale University Press, 1926.

Tillyard, E. M. W. *The Elizabethan World Picture*. New York: Vintage Books, 1961.

Trevelyan, G. M. *History of England: The Tudors and the Stuart Era*. Vol. II. Garden City, New York: Doubleday, 1953.

Wagner, Bernard M. "Manuscript Plays of the Seventeenth Century." *Times Literary Supplement*, October 4, 1934, p. 675.

Warner, George F., and Julius P. Gilson. *Catalogue of Western Manuscripts in the Old Royal and King's Collections*. 4 vols. London: Oxford University Press, 1921.

Webster, John. *The Duchess of Malfi*. In *The Complete Works of John Webster*. Ed. F. L. Lucas. 4 vols. London: Chatto and Windus, 1927.

Webster's Geographical Dictionary. Springfield, Mass.: G. & C. Merriam and Co., 1962.

Werner, Alexander. *Thomas May als Lustspieldichter*. 1894.

Wolfe, Heinrich. *Thomas May's Tragedy of Cleopatra Queen of Ægypt* Strassburg, 1914.

Wright, Louis B., ed. *Advice to a Son: Precepts of Lord Burghley, Sir Walter Raleigh, and Francis Osborne*. Ithaca, N. Y.: Folger Shakespeare Library, 1962.

For Product Safety Concerns and Information please contact our EU representative GPSR@taylorandfrancis.com
Taylor & Francis Verlag GmbH, Kaufingerstraße 24, 80331 München, Germany

www.ingramcontent.com/pod-product-compliance
Lightning Source LLC
Chambersburg PA
CBHW071803300426
44116CB00009B/1191